THE CHRISTIAN
ART OF FORGIVENESS

The Christian
Art *of* Forgiveness

GUIDED REFLECTIONS TO
CULTIVATE A FORGIVING HEART

JAKE MORRILL

ROCKRIDGE
PRESS

Interior and Cover Designer: Michael Cook
Art Producer: Tom Hood
Editor: Crystal Nero
Production Editor: Ruth Sakata Corley

Cover illustration © lietotajs/iStock, 2020

ISBN: Print 978-1-64876-000-6 | eBook 978-1-64739-570-4

R0

To Gus and Juno,
whose lion-heartedness inspires me.

Contents

FORGIVENESS DOES NOT
EXONERATE THE PERPETRATOR.
FORGIVENESS LIBERATES
THE VICTIM.
IT'S A GIFT YOU GIVE YOURSELF.

–BISHOP T. D. JAKES

Introduction

The Lord's Prayer has been good medicine for me through the years. But part of it can get stuck in my throat. "Forgive us our trespasses as we forgive others who trespass against us." Receiving forgiveness—well, that's not so bad. But forgiving those who trespass against me? Every time? Even the ones who violate my dignity and personhood? That's a hard ask. Maybe you can relate.

I don't know why you picked this book up. I can only imagine the pain you've been through. Maybe forgiveness in your life seems out of the question. Maybe you know you've suffered for too long and it's time to get free. As a character in Toni Morrison's novel *Song of Solomon* says, "Wanna fly, you got to give up the [stuff] that weighs you down." Easier said than done! If you're like me, the Fairy Godmother of Forgiveness has yet to arrive with her magic forgiveness dust.

I believe everyone can get free from what's holding them down. Even you. Over the years as a pastor, a therapist, and a United States Army Chaplain, I've seen the power of forgiveness transform countless lives. If you're skeptical, I hear you. Refusing to forgive can be of some benefit, for a while at least. In fact, refusing to forgive is an important part of my own story.

It was a Sunday morning in July 2008, at a summer camp on the outskirts of Asheville, Tennessee. I was talking to some of the staff when my sister called from somewhere chaotic. It took me a minute to comprehend. She was in Knoxville, at the church where we'd grown up. There'd been a shooting. It wasn't clear how many were injured or dead. The church was full of my childhood Sunday School teachers and mentors. Seven of my family members were in the building. They couldn't locate my father.

On the drive back to Knoxville, more information trickled in. They found my father. Safe. In fact, he'd been the first one to tackle the gunman. All my family members were accounted for and unharmed. But two people had died. Several others were injured.

The gunman had left a letter in his truck. Influenced by talk radio, he had sought out those he'd learned to hate with a plan of causing as much harm as he could. Since my childhood church is well-known for including and celebrating people who are LGBTQIA, that's where he went.

Two years before, in Pennsylvania, another gunman had murdered five Amish girls. Many people were inspired by the Amish community's swift and total forgiveness. Now, as the national media descended upon Knoxville, there was the same expectation: that the dramatic arc of this tragedy would only be complete with a satisfying declaration of forgiveness. But the minister, my friend and colleague, Chris Buice, refused.

If he had stood out in front of the church, with all those cameras, and announced blanket forgiveness, he would have been celebrated. The story might have ended up in a feel-good movie. But Chris's job was not to win accolades. It was to be a pastor. What his people needed, at that moment, was time. They needed to honor their grief and anger, and work on feeling safe in this world again.

Protecting those you love can take on many different looks. In August 2008, Chris Buice, under intense pressure, was refusing to forgive. Protecting the rights of his people to work toward their own healing at a pace that was right for them didn't appear like forgiveness. No one will make a movie of the week about it. It wasn't comfortable. But I saw how his actions mattered to people I love. It certainly gave me permission to feel angry, scared, and sad, without racing to declare a forgiveness I didn't yet feel.

The event set loose a wild anger and fear in me. At age 36, I was the minister of a church near where I grew up. Climbing into the pulpit in front of my own congregation the following Sundays,

I scanned the room for attackers. Disagreeing about public matters wasn't new. Worrying about it was. The next time I spoke out about justice would I be risking my life? Or the lives of church members or even my sweet family? Luke 6:28 [NRSV] says, "Bless those who curse you, pray for those who abuse you." But, at the time, I didn't want to bless or pray for anybody like that. I wanted to fight, to make somebody pay. It was clear I needed to get my mind and heart right.

It took me a while, honestly, to start working on forgiveness.

Seven years later, in 2015, my church put out a message in front of our building that said, "Black Lives Matter." Angry phone calls and letters from around our small city poured in. I can't say it was pleasant. But, strangely enough, even when some threats came, there was peace in my heart. The work of forgiveness, years before, had changed me for good. It had set me free from my anger and fear.

I don't know about you, but in my life, I want to fly. To do so, I have to give up what weighs me down. I want *you* to experience that same freedom forgiveness can bring.

How to Use This Book

Forgiveness, like compassion or mercy, is not a single act, but a quality of the heart. Developing it and integrating it into your life is a process. Be gentle with yourself. Give it time. Now and then, you may get stuck. Old feelings might arise. You may even get frustrated—with yourself or with me. That's okay. It's all part of the challenging journey you've been brave enough to undertake.

To engage with this book in a way that's most helpful to you, let me tell you how it's organized. The first chapter, "Cultivating a Forgiving Mindset," is a broad overview. You'll learn what makes forgiveness an art; who, what, and when to forgive; what forgiveness isn't; how to release negativity; about fight or flight; and about the freedom of forgiveness. The following chapters engage a range of different contexts in which you might seek to forgive, all through illustrative stories paired with exercises to try. We'll look at forgiveness applied to relationships between family members. Then, we'll examine forgiveness among friends, forgiveness with colleagues, and forgiveness in the community. Finally, we'll address perhaps the greatest and most complex challenge of all: forgiving oneself.

I've strived to create a clear, simple format. But you're under no obligation to read it straight through. If you're looking to forgive in a friendship, by all means, skip ahead! This book is for you to use in a way you find most helpful to *you*. You may find forgiveness in one area invites awareness about work toward forgiveness in another. The reflections are intended as companions on the road to a forgiving mindset. However, I should be clear: Although I hope the stories are reassuring, reminding you that you're not alone in your struggle, because you are committing to an intentional growth process, it won't be enough to only skim lightly here and there.

Just like having a gym membership won't get you any healthier if you never put in the work, merely owning this book won't produce the effects that you seek. Every chapter is stocked with reflections, each of which includes an actionable prompt or provocative question. I invite you to engage the process of forgiveness by putting it into practice.

Over time, a forgiving heart will become a habit. But for a while it's going to take your focused intention. It's going to take your commitment. If you want forgiveness in your life, it's going to take real practice. I can't make you commit to the practice or make you hang in there when it's hard. But what I can do is pray for you. For your grit. For some grace. And for the peace of a life set to the deep, steady rhythm of your own forgiving heart. I'll pray that all these things fill your life.

CHAPTER 1

CULTIVATING A FORGIVING MINDSET

In this chapter, we'll explore some dimensions of forgiveness: what makes it an art, when and who *not* to forgive, what forgiveness is not, releasing negativity, our innate fight-or-flight response, and what freedom through forgiveness is like. Think of it like creating a foundation for the rest of the book.

What Makes Forgiveness an Art?

Leonardo da Vinci spent almost 14 years perfecting the *Mona Lisa*. My great-uncle John, an amateur painter at age 95, lovingly worked on a portrait of his late wife, my great-aunt Eileen, for five years. He said he'd never quite managed to capture the Eileen he remembered.

That's the nature of art. It's a creative process, born of love. It takes time. We may start with a vision of the finished product, but once we begin, the process is one of unfurling discovery. There's a burst of engagement. Then, we step back. We lean in again, working at this corner, then at that one. The vision of the complete work might be what inspires an artist to start. But the nature of the creative process only reveals the way forward over time.

The same is true of forgiveness. It's a process of discovery. You learn as you go. Forgiveness is not about getting fixed, though. We're not a flat piece of artwork needing a new coat of paint. We're living things, exquisitely and wondrously made. The human body is composed of 30 trillion different cells. Our story is so much more than one thing or another—and certainly more than only the ways we've been harmed. We exist in an ecosystem of relationships and conditions too many to count. So when it comes to needing repair, it's not about getting *fixed*. It's much more complex. It's about getting *healed*.

Every faith recognizes suffering and the need to respond. How they go about forgiveness varies. There is no universal, off-the-shelf, "right" view. As the essayist Susan Sontag wrote, "One cannot be religious 'in general' any more than one can speak language 'in general.' At any given moment, one speaks English or French or Swahili or Japanese, but not 'language.'" So with love and respect for neighbors of other faiths, as we explore the healing art of forgiveness together, we'll draw from the particular wellspring of the Christian faith.

For example, in the Gospel of Matthew 18:21, Peter comes to Jesus and asks, "Lord, if another member of the church sins against me, how often should I forgive? As many as seven times?" To understand Peter's question, it helps to know that the cultural norm of the day was to offer forgiveness up to three times. Already, Peter's proposal of seven was raising the stakes! In reply, Jesus says, "Not seven times, but I tell you, seventy-seven times." It doesn't mean a literal number of times, however, as some people think.

Some people use step counters to make sure to take 10,000 steps every day. Does that sound like you? Well, before you make a spreadsheet to track 77 attempts at forgiveness, I should mention that some translations have Jesus saying, "seventy times seven," or 490. But the number doesn't matter. Jesus isn't telling Peter to literally count 77, or 490, attempts at forgiveness. He's saying something more radical. He's saying, "Peter, stop counting!" He's saying, "Stop keeping score!"

This book is asking you to stop keeping score of the injuries you've suffered. Stop keeping score of the attempts to forgive. Jesus is not saying, "Forget it." Far from it. He's saying forgiveness is not like counting 10,000 steps. For Christians, forgiveness is an art, not a task.

Maybe you're hoping that reading this book can bring healing to a particular wound. Good news: We can do even better than that! The promise of forgiveness, in the Christian tradition, goes beyond a practical method to handle a specific hurt. One who masters the art of forgiveness experiences a fundamental shift, deep within. It can change everything. The forgiving and forgiven heart greets every morning with courage and hope and meets every challenge with ease and with trust.

I don't know your story and all you've been through, but I do know that you're loved by a God who wants you to be free. And I know that forgiveness is the doorway between the suffering you've known and healing that can be yours.

Who, What, and When to Forgive (or Not to Forgive)

What kinds of actions are forgivable? That's a trick question. You don't forgive an action or behavior; you forgive a person. Forgiveness occurs in the context of relationship. This can be confusing, for example, if we think about one spouse forgiving the infidelity of another. Our attention is drawn to the transgression. But forgiveness is not about judgment. It's about how we choose to relate to the other person. Will we seek vengeance? Or will we grant mercy?

If it's people (and not acts) that we forgive, which people do we forgive, and when? In the Christian context, judging someone's worth isn't ours to decide. It's the province of God. We are taught no child of God is beyond our forgiveness. That said, because forgiveness is profoundly personal, it should never be rushed. As the wise old preacher in the Book of Ecclesiastes says, "For everything there is a season and a time for every matter under heaven." So if someone else is eager to hurry you on toward forgiveness, it's your right to refuse. Anger and tears are precious signals that something of great value has been threatened or harmed. Listening to them, we can be reminded of what we cherish and what we'll defend. Once we've learned what our anger and tears have to teach, we can take up the work of forgiveness, at a time we see as right.

Surprisingly, some research says there are people you *shouldn't* forgive. I like to think of it as shouldn't forgive *yet*. In 2010, researchers, led by Laura Luchies at Northwestern University, published the results of four separate studies on the effects of forgiveness on self-respect, titled *The Doormat Effect: When Forgiving Erodes Self-Respect and Self-Concept Clarity*. The researchers concluded that in toxic relationships when one person has less power, and the other person's harmful behavior is frequent and unrelenting, forgiveness may not be an option while the relationship is ongoing. Even when the harmful behavior is clear to both parties, forgiveness can serve to normalize the behavior. The bottom line: **If forgiveness serves to trap you in a destructive cycle, with no signals that the harmful behavior will change, it might be time to develop an exit plan.** Use that elevated anxiety and anger to find safety, and, only once safe, pursue what it would mean to forgive.

Sometimes, no matter one's safety, it seems impossible to forgive. In my observation, this can come from a healthy sense of self-protection or integrity, believing that to forgive is to condone or approve acts of harm. Instead of willing yourself to push through, it may help instead to listen to that resistance, to hear what it has to tell you, what it's trying to protect. The book *Immunity to Change*, by Robert Kegan and Lisa Lahey, can be a helpful resource for gently working with and honoring your own resistance. What I know is that forgiveness is not the decision to surrender your dignity or self-worth. It's the decision of a person with dignity and worth to finally live in peace. You'll know when you're ready.

What Forgiveness Isn't

For a year in the late 1990s, I was in Cape Town, South Africa, spending most days in the informal settlements, or "townships." In those communities, I heard powerful stories of resilience and healing. I heard great pride, as well, in the Truth and Reconciliation Commission, the legal body which adjudicated the many atrocities of the apartheid era. The TRC's work was to create conditions of dialogue that would lead onward toward restorative justice. That level of reconciliation is inspiring. But it's not the same as forgiveness.

Reconciliation takes at least two parties working together. Forgiveness is something you can realize on your own—even when the other party is unapologetic or you're no longer in contact. In Palestine, a few years ago, I met a man who expressed powerful forgiveness for the Israeli soldiers who had killed a family member. There had been no reconciliation. He never talked with those soldiers. But he no longer spent his days nursing his anger for them.

Maybe you thought forgiveness was giving up or not defending yourself. Maybe you feared forgiveness would act as acceptance of bad behavior. It's not. What happened is part of your story. You don't need to forget. But remembering doesn't need to hurt as much anymore.

The forgiving heart comes about through long practice. It's the exact opposite of giving up. It's insisting that what happened will no longer define you. Forgiveness might be in the form of freeing yourself from a destructive relationship. If you are emotionally, physically, or mentally unsafe in your current relationship, and the one who has hurt you hasn't signaled that you will be valued and safe going forward, in a way that you trust, you are under no obligation to stay in that relationship. Forgiveness in that case is leaving and moving on with your life, not staying where destructive behavior will continue.

Releasing Negativity

Each of us has been hurt. Each of us has hurt others. But some people seem trapped in a cycle, causing hurt in almost every relationship they are in. Strange as it seems, hurting others can be a way of defending oneself. If I lash out at someone who seems to care for me, maybe they'll go away, and I won't have to risk being hurt again. Hurt people hurt people.

Sometimes, hurt people end up hurting themselves, too, by punishing themselves with harrowing self-criticism and anger. Lashing out, at ourselves or others, only continues a cycle of pain. It's never constructive. Regardless of what happened, I can't change the past, and I can't change other people. I can only decide how I will respond. Will I end the cycle of pain? Or will I be one of those hurt people who hurt people?

When in South Africa, I was lucky enough to see Nelson Mandela in person, at the presidential inauguration of his successor. As a band played before thousands of people, Mandela danced on the stage, with as much energy as anyone. Even at age 81 he was the embodiment of freedom itself. After 27 years of unjust imprisonment, he had every reason to be bitter. But he made a decision. As he puts it in his autobiography, *Long Walk to Freedom,* "As I walked out the door toward the gate that would lead to my freedom, I knew if I didn't leave my bitterness and hatred behind, I'd still be in prison." Hopefully, we too can learn to identify and break the cycle.

Forgiveness and the Fight-or-Flight Response

Forgiveness affects not only our outlook and our relationships; it affects our physiology. American physiologist Walter Bradford Cannon first described the fight-or-flight response in 1932. Someone experiencing a stress response to a perceived threat will have predictable physical reactions: quickened heart and lung action, constricted blood vessels, and dilation of pupils. Two other physiological responses—tunnel vision and auditory exclusion—mean that our eyes and ears don't take in as much information when we're under stress. Evolutionarily, all those responses are helpful for mammals who find themselves in life-or-death situations. However, as much suffering, anger, or unhappiness as our relationships might bring us, they are rarely a matter of life or death. So our fight-or-flight responses are inappropriate, and can hinder our ability to respond.

Forgiveness and compassion require the opposite of tunnel vision and auditory exclusion. They require us to see a broader view of things; they ask us to listen for more information. Calming ourselves helps us pursue the thoughtfulness required in forgiveness. And greater calm is also one of the rewards of having achieved forgiveness. Research shows that forgiveness can lead to lower blood pressure and levels of stress.

Understanding the physiological underpinnings of forgiveness helps us understand how we think about it, as well. In a situation where you have struggled to forgive, you may see it as an unwelcome dilemma—a fight-or-flight choice between engaging in painful conflict or painful surrender. Forgiveness is neither the anxious responses of "fight" or "flight." Instead, it's a third way, arrived at thoughtfully and diligently, in which less anxiety and anger in our lives is only one of the rewards.

The Freedom of Forgiveness

A photograph from the Vietnam War, taken in 1972, is as famous as it is disturbing. In it, a nine-year-old girl, naked and crying, is running down a road, burned by napalm dropped by American forces. For Americans, the image reinforced the horror of that war. But, for Kim Phuc, it was personal. She was that young girl. The napalm left burns on more than half of her body. Recovery took a long time. In an interview with the Thomson Reuters Foundation, Phuc said, "Living with hate and bitterness almost killed me many times. When I learned to forgive all those who caused my suffering, that was like heaven on earth for me." She credits her Christian faith with her capacity to forgive. Almost 50 years later, she works with children who are victims of war. She also started an organization that works with first responders and military service members who've suffered burns.

Early in life, it was hard for her to look at the famous photograph that captured the depth of her agony. But now she sees it differently. "I realized that picture is a powerful gift for me to work for peace," she says. "To help people. That picture makes awareness to everyone to stop the war, to stop fighting." Kim Phuc couldn't change what happened to her in the past. No one can. But she has utterly transformed her relationship to what happened.

Forgiveness is a choice. No matter what happened to you, it need not define you. Your story isn't over. As long as you're breathing, you've got choices to make. In Deuteronomy 30:15, we read, "See, I have set before you today life and prosperity, death and adversity." Our choice about whether to forgive is not about what happened. It's about how you'll respond. Will you choose life and prosperity? Or death and adversity? As I see it, it's the difference between those who forgive and those who don't. We think we're punishing the other person by holding onto our hurt and resentment, our anger and bitterness. But we're not. As author Anne Lamott puts it, "Not forgiving is like drinking rat poison and then waiting for the rat to die."

Forgiveness is not about the other person. You don't even need to tell them. As Maya Angelou said, forgiveness is "one of the greatest gifts you can give yourself." Imagine yourself transformed—from agony to gratitude, victim to healer, pitied to powerful. Unburdened, at last.

LISTEN. SLIDE THE WEIGHT
FROM YOUR SHOULDERS AND
MOVE FORWARD. YOU ARE AFRAID
THAT YOU MIGHT FORGET,
BUT YOU NEVER WILL.
YOU WILL FORGIVE AND REMEMBER.

–BARBARA KINGSOLVER,
AWARD-WINNING AUTHOR

CHAPTER 2

FAMILY

Conflict in families is as old as the story of Cain and Abel, the children of Adam and Eve in the Book of Genesis. God favored Abel, making Cain jealous enough drive him to murder his brother. His punishment is a life of wandering.

After injury in your family, when the hurt remains raw, you can feel as if you're like Cain, condemned to lead a life that's unmoored. Because, like it or not, you were formed by your family, and express so much from that inheritance in your own life—from the way you take your coffee to the way you cock our head when you laugh—it's never really possible to start over, fresh. Often, people estranged from their families find a pattern of emotional isolation in other settings, as well. In the short term, some distance can help. But in the longer term, leaving family matters unaddressed can mean toting around a lot of unresolved issues well into adulthood, which can hold you back from the meaningful depth in relationships and life that you seek. Although it may be unrealistic to expect the scene from the parable of the Prodigal Son—in which the father races out to greet his wayward child, all tension between them erased—peace is a fruitful path to seek. As you walk that path, you may find greater peace with yourself.

With the stakes often highest in families—between spouses, between parents and children—the wounds can be deeper and take longer to heal. Family relationships can be especially challenging to navigate for a variety of reasons: current or past wounds; generational pain; differing religious beliefs; expected roles; or acceptance based on race, culture, gender, or on who people love.

In cases of abuse, reconciliation may not be possible or even desired. Forgiveness doesn't ask you to subject yourself to further injury. But moving to the other side of the country and changing your phone number, in the end, isn't what frees you. A greater awareness and understanding, and movement toward a less anxious reaction to family members, can.

The Historian Learns a New Story

Marylee is a history professor in Atlanta. Although she's only in her early 30s, it's clear she'll leave a mark in her field. Whether teaching or writing, she exudes the confidence of her education and accomplishment. Not many would guess that, for years, she struggled inside, thinking back on her childhood in rural eastern Kentucky.

"When I was eight," she says, "my dad lost his job. In our community, that wasn't unusual. It's just part of growing up poor. But my dad took it hard. He was a schoolteacher. He didn't want to work at a grocery store. For months, he wouldn't get out of bed. Afterwards, he was like a ghost in the house. He never worked again."

To support the family, Marylee's mother took on three jobs. It fell to Marylee to make supper, wash clothes, and check on her younger brothers' homework. "It just wasn't fair," she says. "I barely had time for friends or for reading—for doing the things a kid should be able to do, growing up. There I'd be, doing chores for hours, and he'd be back in the bedroom, reading a book."

After leaving home, she hardly ever looked back.

Two years ago, back home for a family funeral, Marylee stayed with her father's sister, Aunt Dorothy. After dinner, on the porch, her aunt told stories about when Marylee's father was a boy. There were stories about him winning the county spelling bee. Becoming the valedictorian. Turning down the chance at graduate school when Marylee's mother was pregnant, to take a job teaching back home. Marylee had never known any of it.

"Things can still be awkward," Marylee says now. "I still have some anger. But Aunt Dorothy's stories helped. I now understand some of what it must have been like for him, for things to turn out like they did. The funny thing is, as a historian, I'm trained to dig deeper, to find stories that show a broader context. But it took sitting on the porch with Aunt Dorothy to do that in my own family."

Create in me a clean heart, O God, and put a new and right spirit within me. Do not cast me away from your presence, and do not take your holy spirit from me.

PSALM 51:10-11

CONSIDER THIS

As you think about someone who has caused you pain, reflect on these questions:

1. If you were telling a story of the pain you experienced, when would the events begin? How would beginning the story 10 or 20 years earlier change the story?

2. Who are two or three people in your family whose perspective you value? From a family historian perspective, what stories or information could you glean from conversations with them?

The Queen, Shrunk Down to Size

When Denise was little, a visit from her grandmother was a glamorous affair. After pulling up in her red Cadillac, she would arrange a little cape over her shoulders before making her way up the path, put together from her perfect hairdo to her high heels. It was like a visit from the queen. Her grandmother always had fun gossip to share. Denise loved everything about her visits. But when Denise was 12 years old, their relationship shifted. As Denise grew up, her body filled out. Her grandmother acted like puberty was a personal insult. She began to phone Denise with advice about dieting, warning her about becoming "too fat."

Denise never told her parents about these calls. Confusing as they were, she'd always wanted to be as glamorous as her grandmother. Maybe this guidance would help. During this time, Denise hated her own body. Her weight fluctuated. Her health suffered. She was miserable.

It was only at a family reunion during the summer before her high school senior year, when one of Denise's cousins overheard their grandmother commenting on Denise's eating, that the spell was broken. The cousin told Denise that, to varying degrees, all the girl cousins had been subjected to similar criticism. Some shrugged it off. But two girls had experienced eating disorders and prolonged periods of depression. Denise was able to share her own experience. Her cousin responded, simply, "That's not love. That's abuse."

Denise didn't talk to her grandmother for the next seven years. For a time, she experienced intense anger. She found a therapist and worked through some ingrained issues regarding her body image. A college women's studies course helped her understand her relationship with her grandmother in broader terms of social pressures. And a new church she attended emphasized a message of God's unyielding love for everyone, including her.

When she was 24, Denise saw her grandmother at another family reunion. The woman who had seemed like a queen now appeared tiny and weak, sitting alone in a lawn chair at the edge of everything, scowling at everyone. Denise didn't go to her, but simply observed. From this distance, she could see how unhappy her grandmother was. She thought about God's unconditional love, and imagined how God might love even that tiny, unhappy woman sitting in that lawn chair. It would be a long time before she'd feel comfortable resuming contact with her grandmother. But on that day, at long last, she started to feel free.

Forgiveness brings us closer to those
who have hurt us and helps them to experience
the forgiveness and love of Jesus through
us who forgives them.

—OMOAKHUANA ANTHONIA

TRY THIS

Fritz Perls, the founder of Gestalt therapy, developed an exercise called "The Empty Chair Technique." Set up two chairs and sit in one. Imagine that across from you is your offender. Describe your complaint as if the offender is present. Now stand up and move to the empty chair. Respond to what's just been said from the perspective of the offender. Continue the conversation, moving back and forth between chairs. The objective is to allow different perspectives to engage the situation, and to facilitate the kind of dialogue between them that may or may not be possible in real life. Even imagined conversations, taken sincerely, can promote a greater sense of forgiveness.

Settling Old Debts

In college, John and Rose seemed like the perfect couple—studious, kind, and attractive. Rose marveled at how others spoke of their relationship, telling her it gave them hope. She had always been shy. Now, when she was next to John, she was envied.

But as the years passed, the pressure to publicly perform their perfection was exhausting. When their kids were little, John was in medical school. He was working hard to build their financial future. But he seemed to have no idea what parenting required, and Rose was also holding down her own career as a bookkeeper. She was on double duty, and he was checked out. Now and then, when she let loose a flash of irritation, he'd listen with understanding. But the fundamental imbalance never changed. Her resentment grew.

When the kids were in elementary school, she'd participate in evening open houses and attend plays and recitals alone. A friend gently teased her that she was a widow. As the kids began high school, something shifted: partly because parenting was easier—the kids were more independent—and partly because John's medical practice was thriving; he had hired associates and no longer needed to work around the clock. It was as though, through the fog of all the previous years, they rediscovered each other.

On their evening walks, they shared how things had been for the last 15 years. One evening, Rose poured out her heart, telling John how hard parenting young children had been. John stopped right there, took Rose's hands, and offered the sincerest apology a person could ever want. It seemed he finally understood the impact his career had on his wife.

For years, Rose had fantasized about such a moment. But instead of relief, what surfaced was old anger. It was perplexing. They even discussed it. He asked what else he could do, but she didn't know. All she knew was that she had been numb, but now she felt unsettled.

One afternoon she got an idea. Her bookkeeping software produced templates for creating invoices. She opened one up. In the space for "Payee," she entered John's name. Below, under "Itemized Charges," she wrote up a detailed account of all she'd carried for their family: attended 16 choral recitals alone, kept everyone happy when Dad was three hours late for Sylvie's sixth birthday party, and so forth.

Soon, the invoice was eight pages long. She printed it out and picked up the large stamp on her desk that said, "PAID." Then, reviewing the itemized charges, she marked every page "PAID." She thought about giving it to John. But she realized the document pile wasn't for him. It was for her. So she filed the invoice in among important family papers. And on their walk that evening, she felt as unburdened with John as she had when they met.

Forgiveness is the economy of the heart.
Forgiveness saves the expense of anger,
the cost of hatred, the waste of spirits.

—HANNAH MORE

TRY THIS

Make up your own invoice. Under "Payee," write the name of the one who has caused harm. Under "Itemized Charges," list out what they've done, or the burdens you've carried because of their actions. You can even add a column beside each item for "Costs," describing the actions' impact on your life. You may not be able to stamp "PAID" on each page, as Rose does in the story, but putting your experience in these terms might allow you to see what you'll need to make changes.

Joseph and His Brothers

Sometimes, among siblings it's easy to pick "the favorite," the one who's clearly doted on more by one or both parents. In the Book of Genesis, in the Hebrew Scriptures, there's a family like that. Out of all his children, Jacob loves his 11th son, Joseph, the most. Jacob even gives Joseph a long and much-envied "coat of many colors," without giving his other sons a thing. When he's 17 years old, Joseph dreams that his brothers are bowing down to him. What's worse, as his brothers see it, is that he takes the dreams seriously.

So one day, while Joseph is out tending their sheep, the brothers ambush him, strip him of his fine, colored coat, and throw him into a pit. They intend to kill him, but instead decide to sell him to a passing caravan that is heading toward Egypt. They return home with Joseph's coat as evidence, telling their father a made-up story of his death by animals.

While in Egypt, Joseph's fortunes rise, but a false accusation lands him in prison.

While there, he meets two of Pharaoh's servants. Joseph interprets their dreams accurately. Two years later, when the Pharaoh has a series of troubling dreams, one of the servants remembers Joseph's accuracy and calls him in. Joseph interprets the Pharaoh's dreams to mean that seven years of abundance will be followed by seven years of famine. Consequently, Pharaoh prepares for the famine by storing up grain. When the famine arrives, Egypt is the only nation prepared, thanks to Joseph. His fortunes and stature begin to rise again.

Among the starving who come to Egypt are Joseph's brothers. They don't recognize him. They beg for food to bring home. Their subservience now is the fulfillment of Joseph's earlier dreams. Joseph feels strong emotions and needs to work out what to do with these brothers who had treated him so badly. But so much time has passed. Joseph has changed. Maybe he's less of a peacock than he was before when he wore that coat of many colors. Likewise, he can see that his brothers—who he'd understandably only remembered as cruel—are worried about their families. They're being responsible. It all takes some time to work out, but, in the end, Joseph reveals himself. The brothers are fearful. Yet Joseph has compassion. The family reunites in Egypt, with plenty to eat, with all now forgiven.

He does not deal with us according to our sins,
nor repay us according to our iniquities.
For as the heavens are high above the earth,
so great is his steadfast love toward those who fear him;
as far as the east is from the west,
so far he removes our transgressions from us.
As a father has compassion for his children,
so the Lord has compassion for those who fear him.
For he knows how we were made;
he remembers that we are dust.

PSALM 103:10-14

CONSIDER THIS

1. When Joseph had established himself as an adult, he could more easily forgive his tormenting brothers. In your life, what seemingly unrelated change in conditions has made it (or could make it) easier for you to forgive?

2. Joseph and his brothers reunite around the mission of caring for their father and the whole family. In your family, what larger shared purpose, requiring cooperation, can you imagine would shift how people relate?

An Unwelcome Welcome to a New Land

Surjit Singh Flora, a journalist based in Ontario, Canada, tells a story from when he was a child and his family immigrated to Canada from India. His father had died unexpectedly, and he and his mother and siblings crammed into his aunt's apartment to live with her family. Flora didn't speak English and was overwhelmed by the newness of it all. His aunt only made it worse. It started as teasing, became insulting, then outright bullying. She told his family that they'd never make it in Canada—that they'd always struggle in their new country and they'd only ever know the hard lives of working in a factory.

Flora didn't think much of it, at first. But then he noticed it more and more. In the end, he experienced not only emotional but physical responses to his aunt's bullying. He began to get headaches. His mother tried to intervene, but his aunt's bullying didn't stop. Even after his mother was able to move her family into their own apartment, Flora kept his distance from his aunt for a good five years. His aunt noticed and would complain to his mother and older sister. When they ran into each other at a family event, his aunt approached him, asking, "What have I done?"

Flora replied, "Aunty, I love you and will always have respect for you and your opinions. But in this case, I am finding it very hard to dismiss the nasty comments you made about me and my family. I found I could not let such remarks go. They were hurtful, cruel . . . and though you aimed them to me and my family, I was the one you hurt. I hope that was unintentional."

His aunt apologized. But, as Flora describes it, that alone didn't resolve things. When he thought about her bullying behavior, he wanted to avoid her—or, worse, to get revenge. He knew he wanted to develop a different response—he wanted peace in his heart—but it took time. He learned that forgiveness didn't mean forgetting what had happened or minimizing the pain he had felt. What it meant was that he had worked through the ability of that treatment to continue to hurt him.

As long as you don't forgive,
who and whatever it is will occupy
a rent-free space in your mind.

–ISABELLE HOLLAND

TRY THIS

Take out a piece of clean paper and a pen. On one side of the paper, write down all that you know about the person you're trying to forgive. Include their flaws, their ways of creating pain, and their incapacity for treating others with compassion. Now, turn the paper over. At the top of this opposite side, write, "How God Sees Things." If that perspective is hard to access, and if you are a person who prays, you might pray a little before you do this. Now describe this same person from the perspective as you imagine a loving and merciful God would. For instance, if Flora saw his aunt as a bully, he might imagine God would see the pain within her that contributed to the pain she caused others.

Precious God, I thank You for the power and possibility of forgiveness you have planted in me. Today, I am choosing to use that power to pursue the freedom of forgiveness, especially with regard to [name of the one who hurt you]. As I make that choice, I know it's not easy. So, I'm asking Your help. Be with me, Lord. Keep my heart open when it wants to shut tight. Help me stay the course of my intention, to set free and release [name of the one who hurt you] to Your care. Teach me to move through this world unburdened, with a gentle spirit, with compassion for others as well as myself. Let me grow strong in my vulnerability, trusting in You alone, as I re-dedicate the temple of my heart through the cleansing power of forgiveness.

All this I pray, in Your holy name.

Amen.

The Long Homecoming

Only three weeks after they celebrated their 10th anniversary, Yasmin gave Tim the surprise of his life. Not the good kind. Lying in bed one night, she murmured, "I've got something to tell you. I don't want to. But I have to."

For three months the year before, she had carried on an affair with a man at work. Her voice quavered. She begged Tim to forgive her. She loved raising their kids together with him. She was proud of who he was, and said she wanted to grow old together. But Tim was so upset he could hardly register anything that she said. He went to sleep on the living room couch. For weeks, they barely spoke to each other. They shared chores, but in silence.

In a way, they were more comfortable sharing duties than they were sharing what was in their hearts. Tim was a Sergeant Major in the Army Reserve. Over the years, he'd been deployed three times to Afghanistan. While separated, Tim and Yasmin's communication became businesslike. There was never a joyful reunion when Tim came home from deployment. Things were awkward. Tim was more comfortable playing video games than he was engaging in what he called "idle chit-chat." He had stories from down range, combat stories of losing buddies through hours of chaos, that he never wanted to share. Among the soldiers he knew who'd come back from multiple deployments, a lot more of their marriages had fallen apart than had continued.

After two months, Tim shared the situation with one of his best friends. The friend recommended that Tim talk to a Chaplain, who referred him to a therapist specializing in military personnel. Over a few sessions, Tim came to see a bigger picture. He saw how hard his absence was on his family, and even harder when he returned. He was like a puzzle piece from a different puzzle, always trying to fit in. He wanted to talk about how angry he was with Yasmin, but the therapist encouraged him to focus on himself, on his choices. Gradually,

Tim saw how video games kept him at a distance from Yasmin. He could start to see how she might have hungered for the attention of someone, even a colleague at the office.

There came the night when, with tears in his eyes, he asked Yasmin to forgive him for hiding in video games instead of facing up to how hard it was to come home. He said he wanted to stop blaming her. It still took a long time for Tim and Yasmin to build trust in each other. They knew it would take work and forgiveness from both to come back home to each other.

As God's chosen ones, holy and beloved, clothe yourselves with compassion, kindness, humility, meekness, and patience. Bear with one another and, if anyone has a complaint against another, forgive each other; just as the Lord has forgiven you, so you also must forgive.

COLOSSIANS 3:12-13

TRY THIS

When we've been injured emotionally, we can fall prey to imagining ourselves as blameless. We can overlook the times we've injured others. The invitation in this exercise is to do otherwise: to meditate on how you've hurt others, even unintentionally. Looking back on your life, see if you can make a list of 25 times you have offended or injured others. Such a list won't erase the real harm you have suffered. But looking at our own failings can help shift our view away from the concept of "good people" and "bad people." Humans are complex. We have *all* fallen short of God's perfect love.

A Reunion in Prayer

Holly worked as a reference librarian at the medical school. She had a devoted and funny boyfriend, Miguel. She had a circle of friends. At 27, by all appearances, she was thriving. But all of that couldn't erase the sorrow she felt regarding her father.

Growing up, Holly and her dad had a special relationship. They went fishing. They were part of a crew from church that did fix-it projects for elderly people. With her confidence in public speaking, a lot of people assumed that Holly would go into the ministry, and probably be a preacher somewhere. Her dad was especially proud of that.

But when Holly came out as a transgender woman at age 20, all of that stopped. Her dad could barely look her in the eye. Yes, he called her by her new name, Holly. He'd even shared a meal when she brought Miguel home to introduce him around. But the old warmth and ease was gone. She had tried to talk with him about it, but he always waved it off, muttering something about maybe being old-fashioned, before shutting completely down. He wasn't one to talk about his deep feelings.

One night, home on the couch with a movie, Holly's phone rang. It was her dad. In halting words he said he'd been reading on the Internet about transgender people and Christianity. He had assumed that to be transgender was to go against Christ. That's all he'd ever heard, anyway. But now he found some websites that looked at things differently—like the story from the Book of Acts, where one of the first converts to the early Christian Church was an Ethiopian eunuch. One theory is the word "eunuch" means something like being transgender. For years, her dad said, he'd been at war with himself. He still had a lot to learn, but just wanted to tell her that he was doing some reading and thinking and was seeing that it was possible to love God and to love Holly, too. In fact, he could see that by withholding love for his own child, he had refused to love God, as well. This was more than

Holly had ever heard her dad speak in one stretch. It seemed like he was crying. They both were.

Then, something even more unexpected happened: He asked if she'd lead them in prayer. Holly had always prayed, but it had been a long time since she had prayed out loud. But the words came swiftly to her. Even over the phone, she felt God between her and her dad. She asked for mercy and grace, and the courage to be honest in speaking from the heart.

Two years after that, Holly married Miguel. Her dad, tears of pride and joy rolling over his cheeks, walked his daughter down the aisle.

> *Forgiving is certainly one of the greatest human capacities and perhaps the boldest of human actions insofar as it tries the seemingly impossible, to undo what has been done, and succeeds in making a new beginning where everything seemed to have come to an end.*
>
> —HANNAH ARENDT

TRY THIS

See what taking your situation to prayer can yield. Try praying for your own healed heart. Pray for understanding. Pray for patience. Whatever it is you might need in your process, see what can happen when you ask for God's ongoing assistance in doing the hard work of forgiveness.

The Fumbled Hand-Off

Darla started out in an entry-level job and became a success in the insurance business. As she liked to tell it, her first position was as a receptionist who didn't know how to type. But she stayed up late every night, practicing. Her gumption was noticed. She climbed through the ranks and became an insurance salesperson, eventually starting her own firm.

In her late 50s, looking ahead at retirement, she had the perfect plan. Her daughter, Candice, had never really settled on a career. But she was good with people. With some training and development, Candice would be the perfect person to take over the firm. Although only lukewarm about the idea, Candice agreed. Darla pursued the transition, funding business courses and introducing her to her contacts around town. She even bought space on four local billboards. Both of their faces were on it, along with the tagline, "Generation to generation, a family name you can trust."

Several months after Darla's 60th birthday, she took Candice out to lunch. She told her daughter she was getting ready to hand over the reins. It was only then, after more than three years of training and preparation, that Candice told her she had been thinking of moving to Florida to start a new life.

Darla felt everything she had worked for slipping through her fingers. She was furious. Other high-achieving employees could have been cultivated to take over the business, but Darla had cleared the way for her daughter. She stormed out of the restaurant. A few months later, Candice moved to Florida.

Darla didn't think there was time to develop a smooth transition to anyone else, so over the next year, she sold her business to a national company and retired to a small apartment downtown. She waited a couple of years for Candice to apologize for misleading her, but the call never came. Candice seemed to be just as hapless in Florida as she had been before. Darla realized, over time, that she'd have to come to accept the daughter she had, not the daughter she wanted.

Before we can forgive one another,
we have to understand one another.

—EMMA GOLDMAN, EARLY ACTIVIST AND WRITER

CONSIDER THIS

1. An old folktale has a snake convincing a passerby to pick it up. The passerby refuses, but the snake persists. Finally, the passerby relents and picks up the snake, whereupon the snake bites him. The passerby complains, but the snake only says, slithering away, "You knew I was a snake when you picked me up." Think about the situation in which you're considering forgiveness. From the right angle, could you have predicted the harmful behavior from the person at fault, knowing them to be nothing other than who they are?

2. In a similar light, looking back, are there ways you imagined or pretended that things were other than they were? Not that what happened was your fault! You may have been slow to see it because you were invested in seeing things a different way. As you learn to trust again, how can you see things as they are, and not as you wish they were?

Inheriting Impatience and Anger

When my grandfather, Whitey, was nearing the end of his life, my father and I visited him in his mobile home park. The relationship between Whitey and my father was never easy. That weekend, I caught a glimpse of some of it. By this point in his life, Whitey didn't move around much. When my father got up to get some milk from the fridge, and chose the wrong glass for his father, Whitey barked at him from across the room, "No, not that one!" My dad, otherwise confident, froze. It reminded me of how he could be impatient with me, and how I can sometimes get with my own kids. I had the inkling that whatever this tendency was went back farther than Whitey.

Sure enough, my dad told me that Whitey had been the first-born son of a farmer in rural Iowa with a harrowing temper. If something went other than planned, that farmer would go off, shouting and looking for a switch to hit his kids. From what I could tell, it must have been a miserable childhood for Whitey. Even if he was sometimes explosive in his impatience, maybe Whitey doing the best he could. The same with my own dad. And the same with me.

It seemed like this angry energy, this impatience, was part of my inheritance. Each generation was doing what they could to pass a little less of it down the line. At some point in my 40s, I became interested in genealogy, and began to construct a heavily annotated family tree. During this family research, I happened upon some documents online regarding my great-grandfather, that angry farmer in rural Iowa. The documents didn't tell the story of the terrifying wild man I'd heard about. They touted his good character and responsibility in handling some difficult family business during a hard year for the crops. This sober character, able to be trusted, was a different person than the one I'd imagined, and heard stories about, for so long.

I still believe the stories about his temper. Four generations of impatience and angry energy in the men in our family didn't come out of nowhere. But getting a glimpse of a different side of him made me wonder what else I had never considered. Maybe we inherited some good things, too.

Without forgiveness life is governed
by an endless cycle of resentment
and retaliation.

−ROBERTO ASSAGIOLI, ITALIAN PSYCHIATRIST

CONSIDER THIS

1. When one has experienced injury, it can make sense to respond with emotion: to feel the feelings deeply. At the same time, as we move toward healing, thinking can play a part, too. Not only ruminating, but learning. In that spirit, what new information could you learn about the situation or person who has injured you? Can you find 25 new relevant facts you never knew before?

2. Being troubled by what has happened can stop our curiosity or openness to new perspectives on it. If you accept that you don't yet know the full story, or have all the information, what are 10 new questions you could ask?

A Story with No Villains

Priscilla's mother died five years after treatment for cancer. Her father, George, was a devoted caregiver. He sobbed at the memorial. But, three months later, George was already in a serious relationship with a woman named Abigail. Things were not easy with her. Priscilla's family had always liked watching comedies, but Abigail preferred quiet, so George said that's what he preferred. The family had always made a big deal out of the holidays, overdecorating their parents' house and loudly singing carols. But Abigail was uncomfortable with so many people in the house, so they canceled Christmas that year. Priscilla and her sister, Dawn, began to wonder: What was Abigail's problem? Why was she so uptight? Had she put a spell on their father? He had always been so tenderhearted and ready for a laugh. But now he'd grown serious.

The sisters tried to develop a relationship with phone calls to the house, but Abigail would stay on the phone only a minute or two before calling for George. They asked if Abigail would like to join them for a weekend in the city or go to an art museum, which was the kind of thing Abigail seemed to like. But whatever they suggested, she declined.

It seemed like she was committed to sucking the joy out of life, and out of the life of their father as well. He chided them now, when they'd visit, for talking too loudly, reminding them that Abigail liked to keep a quiet house. Already, they'd struggled with the loss of their mother. Now, it seemed, they'd lost their father, as well. One afternoon Priscilla was on a tear, mocking Abigail for her sensitive ways. Priscilla's husband, Roger, listened—he had heard much of it before and kept quiet. But now he said gently, "You know, it's not all Abigail. Your father's a grown man. He's made some different choices. He's part of this, too. Every one of us is. For all I know, maybe even including your mother. It's more complicated than just Abigail." Priscilla had to admit she may have been too quick to place blame.

[Genesis 1] talks about night and day and land and water, but we have dusk and we have marshes. These verses don't mean 'there's only land and water, and there's nowhere where these two meet.' These binaries aren't meant to speak to all of reality—they invite us into thinking about everything between and beyond.

—M BARCLAY

TRY THIS

We know about ecosystems in nature—how different elements in a complex system relate to one another and play a part in sustaining the whole. But we think less often about how this could be true in human dynamics. Sometimes, we imagine that one particular person is acting on their own in harmful ways, without noticing or naming how others enable or even participate in what's happening. In this exercise, write down at least seven people connected to your situation. For each person, write at least three ways in which they have contributed or played a part.

"A happy marriage," wrote American humorist Robert Quillen, "is the union of two good forgivers." More trenchantly, movie star Marlene Dietrich said, "Once a woman has forgiven her man, she must not reheat his sins for breakfast." Whatever the configuration of our families, if we're to share daily life with each other, the ongoing practice of forgiveness is essential. Marriage researcher John Gottman has studied couples' interactions for almost five decades, learning some of the qualities that ensure resilience. One is what he calls the habit of "repair." A repair, as Gottman sees it, isn't a quick fix. Instead, it's anything that one or both partners do to stop a negative interaction from spiraling out of control. It could be a humorous remark. It could be a tender word. A repair conveys that, whatever the misstep, the marriage rests on a foundation that's stronger and broader than anything wrong. This, too, is the orientation of the forgiving heart: to forever point to the broader context of love and appreciation (an inevitable stubbed toe notwithstanding).

IT IS EASIER TO FORGIVE AN ENEMY THAN IT IS TO FORGIVE A FRIEND.

—WILLIAM BLAKE, POET

CHAPTER 3

FRIENDS

Even before you left your childhood home, maybe as early as in the sandbox, you may have found companions for the journey of life. Close friends can understand you and your views even more than your family. For some people, life includes relationships with both family and friends. For others, friends become a "chosen family" with all the fixings: holiday meals, hospital visits, and caregiving. Over time, friendship can become a precious vessel containing memories, shared understandings, and the deep acceptance of intimacy. These relationships know peaks, but also valleys. Moments of misunderstanding. Inevitable incidents of irritation. Fans of the Harry Potter series will remember the moment when professor Albus Dumbledore praises student Neville Longbottom. "There are all kinds of courage," said Dumbledore, smiling. "It takes a great deal of bravery to stand up to our enemies, but just as much to stand up to our friends." Oftentimes, forgiveness in friendship requires facing the hard truth. It demands both parties name the pain between them, taking the risk that either friend could simply walk away.

Conflict or wounds in a friendship can come about through clashing values, a genuine misunderstanding, or unmet needs. They can be rooted in different expectations of roles, or different views on important topics. People of different genders and cultures can experience friendship differently or bring a different framework of understanding to the relationship. The alliance formed between strangers that grows into friendship can be fraught with peril if its rooted in the assumption that friends can never disagree. However, friends who have dared to develop the heart of forgiveness will find the bravery of honesty has rewarded them with richer connections, at a greater depth than a relationship committed to mere harmony and peacekeeping. If you have been hurt by someone you considered a friend, this chapter is for you. You'll find narratives that explore that experience from different angles; all of them encouraging a response from a heart of forgiveness.

Would You Rather Be Loving, or Would You Rather Be Right?

Sarah and Bethany had first become friends as young moms at the playground, watching over their kids. Sarah liked Bethany's slow drawl and sly wit. Bethany liked Sarah's frank opinions on everything from wine to politics to the best shade of blue for an afternoon sky.

One day, Bethany had been hemming and hawing over buying a car. It was used, she said, and the price was right. Then again, she mused, maybe the high mileage meant expensive repairs up ahead. Something about the meandering nature of Bethany's decision-making set Sarah off. If Bethany couldn't make a decision, Sarah was just going to make it for her. In a crisp, five-minute speech, Sarah told Bethany exactly how to handle the purchase—how much she should haggle, what kind of insurance to buy, everything down to the final detail. As Sarah saw it, this advice was a tremendous gift. But as she finished, she noticed the look on Bethany's face was something other than grateful.

"Are you kidding?" Bethany burst out. "Do you think I'm a child, talking to me like that?"

Sarah said, with irritation, "I was just trying to help."

That night, Bethany told her wife, Heidi, about the conversation with Sarah. Heidi said, "Well, as I see it, you could end your friendship with Sarah, or you could be brave and tell her how it felt, and what you'd like from her in the future."

That only made Bethany mad. "Sheesh," she said. "Everyone's got advice."

Bethany decided to continue meeting up with Sarah, but with some coldness now. She was almost 40 years old. She wasn't going to be treated like a child! She'd teach Sarah a lesson about trying to push other people around! Heidi called it Bethany's "walls up" position, where she seemed to be her usual friendly self, but with some distance and guardedness.

Sarah could sense it. She even guessed it had something to do with their conversation about the used car. But she wasn't going to apologize for trying to help. Bethany was just being oversensitive, Sarah figured.

One Sunday, when Bethany and Heidi were at church, the sermon included the question, "Would you rather be loving, or would you rather be right?" Driving home, Bethany admitted that she was tired of maintaining the "walls up" stance with Sarah. She didn't want to have a big conversation about who had been right. All she wanted was to let go of the anger and love her friend Sarah again. She dialed up Sarah's number and said, "Hey, friend. I'd love to go and get coffee with you." It was like the ice melted. The impasse was over. The messiness where love in friendship is found would carry on like it always had. Both friends were happy.

When you forgive, you love. And when you love,
God's light shines upon you.

–JON KRAKAUER, AUTHOR

CONSIDER THIS

1.   Think about the challenge, "Would you rather be loving, or would you rather be right?" Each has its merits. What's the answer for you, and when?

2.   How can you tell if you're trying to be right versus trying to be loving? Sometimes, the loving thing is to hold others accountable. If that's true, how do you know when your desire to be loving isn't just stubborn?

Walking Humbly with Your God

Todd and Omar both worked in management at a manufacturing plant outside Lexington, Kentucky. They became friends by making faces at each other during long, boring meetings. They soon found they had a lot in common. They loved Kentucky basketball and loved hip-hop. But there were differences, too. The biggest was religion. Todd attended a nondenominational church in downtown Lexington. Omar went to the masjid, or mosque.

Todd had never met someone who was Muslim before, so he peppered Omar with questions. Omar would say, "Look, man, I'm not an expert, but it's like this," and he'd explain Islam in a way that fascinated Todd. Omar had lived in Kentucky his whole life and had met plenty of Christians, but he appreciated the open-hearted and enthusiastic way that Todd talked about his faith.

On the weekends they played pick-up basketball. One Saturday, Todd invited Omar to his parents' house for a pool party. Todd's family was delighted to meet his friend from work. Now and then, Todd's father would make the rounds with a platter of hot dogs and hamburgers. Omar, having a great time, declined every time.

Finally, Todd called, "Hey, bro! Don't insult the man of the house. Have a burger!" He said it in a joking tone, but it was serious, too. In Todd's family, a polite guest would have accepted the offer of food graciously.

Omar laughed it off. Todd made up a burger for Omar anyway, and brought it over to him "Eat, bro," he said. "These are so good."

But Omar waved him off. "Hey, I'm sure they are. But, you know, *halal* and all." Omar explained that he only ate meat that was *halal*—prepared in a certain way, by a certified butcher. Todd was so anxious that his parents would judge the strange ways of his guest that he hissed, "C'mon. I won't tell."

Omar was used to living around Christians who didn't understand Islam or didn't respect it. But he'd thought Todd was different. He left soon after, upset.

As for Todd, he didn't know what to make of it. He had thought Omar was so laid back. Now, he was hung up on how the meat was prepared? Maybe they didn't have as much in common as he had thought.

The next Monday, Todd asked Omar to meet outside during lunch. He said, "Look, man. I don't know what happened Saturday, but it ended weird. I probably messed up. But if we're going to be friends, it's going to have to include a lot of messing up. I'm sorry. I love me some Jesus. But I also love me some Omar. So I'm going to keep learning about Islam, if you're willing to teach me."

He has told you, O mortal, what is good;
and what does the Lord require of you
but to do justice, and to love kindness,
and to walk humbly with your God?

MICAH 6:8

CONSIDER THIS

1. Have you had a friendship go off the rails because of cultural or religious differences? If so, were you able to successfully navigate those differences? How?

2. Think of important relationships in your life, especially across differences of culture or religion. Consider three steps you could take to broaden your understanding and deepen your compassion. Examples include watching movies or reading books centering on that culture's perspective, attending a worship service as a guest, and doing online research.

Breaking Up with a Friend

Dan and Jimmy became friends in their 40s. Like a lot of married straight men, outside of socializing as couples with his wife, Dan hadn't made a new friend on his own since college. And Jimmy was a good one—always sharing something profound he'd just read and asking good questions. But there was a shadow to this friendship because something in Jimmy's marriage was off. At first, he reported, they were working on it. But over a year, things were starting to head south.

Jimmy began to call Dan more often. No more talk about books or big questions. Now, it was only Jimmy's voice on the phone, crackling with stress, as he weighed what to do. Dan had a reputation as a good listener. After all the insight he'd received from Jimmy, maybe taking some time to listen was a contribution to the friendship that Dan could make.

Then one day Jimmy called, frantic. The story came out. For months, Jimmy had carried on an affair with a woman at work. His wife found out. Things were out of control. During one of those calls, Dan realized that this friendship no longer brought him joy. He dreaded talking to Jimmy, which was confusing. Was Dan a fair-weather friend, only in it for the good times? Dan considered himself understanding and open. But he had to admit, the idea that Jimmy had cheated on his wife, and seemed not to understand the impact, rankled Dan. He didn't want to be a prude. But it was hard to trust someone who'd been managing so many half-truths. Dan intended to share his feelings the next time Jimmy called. But Jimmy was talking a blue streak. He was in no condition to listen.

After they hung up, Dan was furious. He felt used. Opening his laptop, he typed out a message about how their talks had become Jimmy's extended complaint sessions. Dan said he was sorry that Jimmy's marriage was falling apart, but he couldn't be his therapist.

After typing for 30 minutes, he pushed "Send." And immediately regretted it. Lashing out wasn't his way. But he didn't know what else to do. Twenty minutes later, his phone started ringing. Dan didn't pick up. After that, the two men didn't talk for a very long time.

Two years later, they ran into each other at the neighborhood swimming pool. By then, Jimmy had been through a lot of therapy and moved into a new chapter of life. Dan had come to realize how his own failure to speak up and set boundaries, not to mention his self-righteousness, had played a part in the situation. Jimmy and Dan never rekindled the friendship they'd had. But, even without saying as much, the brief encounter at the pool let both of them know forgiveness was offered and accepted.

> *We are not at peace with others because*
> *we are not at peace with ourselves,*
> *and we are not at peace with ourselves*
> *because we are not at peace with God.*
>
> –THOMAS MERTON, CATHOLIC PRIEST AND MYSTIC

TRY THIS

On a piece of paper, write out four or five life stages you've been through. For each, write the names of your closest friend in that stage. Unlike Jimmy and Dan's friendship, have you had friendships that survived an especially challenging life-stage transition (graduation, marriage, childbirth, divorce, retirement, and so forth)? If so, what did you do to help the friendship weather that storm? The answer might contain resources for ways to practice forgiveness that you've already successfully implemented!

Across the Social Media and Partisan Divide

Angela and Shelby were best friends in high school but drifted apart. It was only at their 20th reunion that they reconnected. They both had kids, had gone through divorces, and were now living near where they had grown up. A little tipsy from the refreshments at the reunion, they pledged to see each other again soon. But as so often happens, they didn't. They were able to connect through social media, and started to engage with each other almost daily. Angela would "like" Shelby's pictures of her kids. Shelby commented on a post Angela made about enjoying a walk outdoors. Their interactions were never all that substantial, but it was nice to be in touch. The next year, all of that changed.

It was an election year, and Shelby's brother, Douglas, who'd been such a pest in high school, was now just as opinionated online. Shelby seemed to ignore him, but Angela just couldn't. She began to reply to Douglas, sometimes sarcastically. It started out in fun—after all, she could hardly believe he was no longer 14 years old. But their political disagreements were intense. And neither one could seem to back down from a fight. One day, Angela tagged Shelby on a post Douglas made and said, "Come get your brother. He's at it again." Angela didn't check Facebook for several hours. When she did, she was shocked. Her friend, Shelby, had let loose a tirade about Angela and "all those other people like you." Angela hadn't realized that she and Shelby were so far apart in their political views. Angela typed out a snarky reply. A few minutes later, here came Shelby again. Back and forth they went.

The next day, Angela had a dilemma. She knew she'd been out of line. Then again, so had Shelby. Angela stewed on it a few days. She didn't believe in playing nice; she valued honesty. But part of what broke her heart about the country was how politics could ruin relationships. She was committed to not getting trapped in that rut.

A few days later, Shelby received flowers at her home, with a note from Angela. It said, "In high school, we vowed that we were going to do great things in the world. I don't know whether we have. But, if we can stay friends, even through our disagreements, I think we'll be making the world a little more loving. I'm not going to talk politics on social media with you or your brother again, but if you want, I'll hear you out in person (and promise to listen). Mostly, though, I want to know about your kids and what you hope for and are working for in your life. Even when we believe our politics are a matter of life and death, I want our friendship to rest in a love bigger than how we will vote."

> *To forgive is to set a prisoner free and discover that the prisoner was you.*
>
> —LEWIS B. SMEDES, CHRISTIAN AUTHOR AND THEOLOGIAN

CONSIDER THIS

1. How do you understand your in-person relationships differently from your online relationships? Do you have different expectations and boundaries for each?

2. In political disagreements, people can dehumanize those with other beliefs and identities, especially when it's easier to say things online than to say them in person. How can you remain compassionate for others across the divide? How can you see them from angles beyond the political context? What competing values does your faith require of you in that moment—and how do you decide to act?

Betrayed by the Book Club

When Cindy and her husband moved to a new town for his job, she had felt so alone. Now, after a year, she looked forward to her Wednesday night book club. No matter the book, the group of five women always found a way to connect it to their own experiences. She shared parts of her life she had never shared with anyone other than her own husband, and could count on her "sisters" nodding in understanding. But, gradually, attendance began to falter. Instead of five, they'd be only three or four in the room. By Thanksgiving, the group petered out. There were some tears at the last meeting, as the members of the group expressed appreciation for one another. As for Cindy, she felt bereft.

Everyone pledged to find ways to stay connected. But in February, sitting by herself in the elementary school assembly hall for her kid's open house, she overheard a conversation that gave her a jolt. Two women behind her were happily chatting. Cindy didn't mean to eavesdrop, but she couldn't help but overhear. As it turned out, the two women were in a new book club. As Cindy kept listening, she learned that it included three of the members of her former book club. The group had started in January. They were reading one of the books that the old book club had planned to read. It was all Cindy could do to hold back the tears.

Over the next weeks, Cindy replayed the last meetings of the book club in her mind. She tried to think of signs that the group members were connecting with one another to cut her out. But she could think of nothing. She had fantasies of showing up unannounced at the new book club, with her own copy of the book, or of confronting one of the new group's members. But, for now, she thought that what she needed to do was to take some long walks. So that's what she started to do Wednesday evenings. Those walks gave her time to think—and, sometimes, to cry. Week after week, on these walks, she got stronger.

Her view softened. Honestly, there had probably been times in her own life when she had been deceptive and distanced herself from others without saying why. And, anyway, their betrayal at the end didn't erase the genuine experience of care she had felt in the book club's first year. Eventually she stopped harboring fantasies of bursting in and embarrassing everyone. Instead, she began to think of how the experience could make her a better friend to others—such as what she could learn about honesty and directness. After some time, she even began to wish each of the other members well.

> *There are moments when one has to*
> *choose between living one's own life,*
> *fully, entirely, completely—or dragging*
> *out some false, shallow, degrading existence*
> *that the world in its hypocrisy demands.*

—OSCAR WILDE, *LADY WINDERMERE'S FAN*

TRY THIS

In this exercise, I invite you to write a series of sincere blessings for the person who hurt you. Knowing the person as you do, what opportunities or changes would bless them and those around them? See if you can write down at least 10.

God of our hearts, and of the generations,

Of Abraham, Sarah, and Hagar,

We give thanks for all You have provided us in this life,

Especially, today, the companions for our journey:

The ones who know our stories,

Who remember what's important to us,

Who honor our personhood.

Lord, sometimes, this journey together with

friends can be painful,

And this is one of those days.

We come before you with hurting hearts,

With pain and confusion,

With doubt and despair.

It's so hard to trust when we've been treated like this.

But we know that we don't want to be held

In the cage of un-forgiveness.

As hard as it is, and as unwilling as we may be

in our bitterness,

Teach us Your ways. Fill us with Your spirit.

Help us come back to the path of friendship

With a forgiving heart. No longer allowing the

pain of the past

To hold us back from the purpose You have

in mind for us.

Let us do Your will and help create heaven on earth,

Especially, today, in our friendships.

All this we pray, in Your holy name,

Amen.

Calling Time-Out

Trey and Diane had known Steve and Jackie for eight or nine years. They'd met at a neighborhood meeting and had all hit it off. Trey and Jackie were storytellers and wisecrackers. Their spouses were quieter, enjoying it all. They started the tradition of an annual camping trip each October. One year in September, when Trey called up to check in on the plans for the trip, Steve was evasive. He said he and Jackie weren't going to go on the trip that year. Trey was shocked. This was something they looked forward to every year. When Diane called the next week to see if they wanted to go to a movie, again Steve was quiet on the phone, offering up weak excuses. Trey and Diane were baffled.

A week later, a letter arrived. Jackie said she needed to take a break from their friendship. She'd been angry for months. It went back to April, when her mother had died in a car accident. At the time, Trey and Diane were attentive, bringing food over and even hosting a "bad movie" night. But, as Jackie saw it, all that care and attention had gone away as quickly as it had appeared. Within a month, as she was still deeply grieving her mother, Trey and Diane seemed to only want to talk about hiking trips and the ridiculous hairstyle of the sports anchor on the local channel. It had been like they'd forgotten her loss.

Trey and Diane were horrified. They thought they'd been trying to lighten the load for her, to liven things up in a sad year. But they could see her point. They could have asked about her mother or checked in on her more. They drove over to Steve and Jackie's house. When they showed up, Steve wouldn't let them in. "Sorry, guys," he told them. "She's just going to need time."

Trey had always been popular—and was accustomed to making things better with a joke or a witty remark. Diane, was skilled at her genuine compassion to connect with people, to hear them out, and to let them know they were understood. What to do now?

Meanwhile, Jackie spent several weeks at home, thinking. She came to see that the break from Trey and Diane was less about her friends' behavior and more about her own need for solitude in her grief. She also realized, to her chagrin, that she had expected Trey and Diane to read her mind.

Around Christmas, Jackie visited Trey and Diane and told them everything. She said she forgave them for not following up and checking in on her grief. But, more than that, she asked if they'd forgive her, for not being clear enough about what she needed. The friends hugged. The following year's camping trip was the best one yet.

A broken friendship that is mended through forgiveness can be even stronger than it once was.

—STEPHEN RICHARDS

CONSIDER THIS

1. Think of a relationship that is currently causing you strife. If you could call a time-out to have the time and space to heal, how much time would you need? Why?

2. If you had a break from a friendship, what are some things you could do to facilitate healing? If miscommunication was a factor, you could learn about effective communication. If conflict played a part, consider exploring conflict resolution. A renewed focus on your own well-being during this time could also include adopting a sustainable spiritual practice or clarifying your goals about the friendship.

Deciding What to Remember

Carl and Rusty had been friends for six years through a community program called "Bridge-Builders," which facilitated relationships between neurotypical people and people with intellectual disabilities. Carl's caseworker, Pam, made all the arrangements. She was good at setting things up, and then stepping back. Carl loved getting out of the group home twice a month and relating with people other than his family. Rusty got a kick out of Carl's zest for life.

Carl lived in a home with other residents who had intellectual disabilities. A born extrovert, he loved country music and going to the aquarium. Rusty was a lawyer. Although he was regarded as neurotypical, Rusty's attention-deficit/hyperactivity disorder (ADHD) made ordinary life challenging. He regularly forgot important obligations. He misplaced court documents. He lost track of time. He'd learned ways to cope but keeping appointments and a routine was a struggle.

One Saturday, Pam shared the news: She was moving out of state. Carl would have a new caseworker. "Gordon," sneered Carl. "He doesn't do anything."

Pam said, "C'mon, Carl. Give him a chance."

"He doesn't do anything," Carl repeated.

Sure enough, in the next few weeks, Gordon didn't call Rusty to set up an outing. Rusty meant to give a call but kept forgetting. Finally, Gordon set up an outing—a visit to a park. But it was the beginning of the end. Pam's ability to organize the outings had been the linchpin of Rusty and Carl's friendship. In the months that followed, Rusty called a few times, but like so many other things, the friendship slid out of his ADHD mind.

Carl's parents set him up with a therapist who helped him express his feelings of loss, both for his caseworker Pam and his friend, Rusty. Carl was able to talk about how confusing and hurtful it was to have important relationships end abruptly. In one session, his therapist prompted Carl to draw a picture of Pam and Rusty as he wanted to remember them. Carl drew a picture of the time they went to an arcade and laughed their heads off. He drew cartoon bubbles with the word "Ha!" over their heads. And then, in the corner, he drew a little black squiggle.

"What's that?" the therapist said.

"That's the sad part," said Carl. "I mostly want to remember the good day. But the sad part, missing them, will also go there."

'Truly I tell you,' Jesus said, 'this very night, before the rooster crows, you will disown me three times.' But Peter declared, 'Even if I have to die with you, I will never disown you.' And all the other disciples said the same. [Later, Jesus] returned to his disciples and found them sleeping. 'Couldn't you men keep watch with me for one hour?' he asked Peter.

THE GOSPEL OF MATTHEW 26:34-40

TRY THIS

Think of a friendship for which you have unresolved pain. On a piece of paper, draw a picture of the memories of that friendship at its best—the parts you would like to remember. Spend time adding vivid detail, to the point the picture takes shape not only on the paper, but also in your memory. See if the positive memories can remain alongside or even eclipse the images of whatever went wrong.

Learning to Take Stock

Sometime in college—no one remembered when—the gang had started what they called "the infinite text." A few times a week, someone would text a picture of a cute dog or a comment about a boring meeting at work. Light stuff. It had been going on for 10 years.

Christine didn't always check the text chain. It made for pleasant background noise in her busy life, with a job, a marriage, and a one-year-old son. One day, though, she happened to read a stray note: "Don't tell Christine!"

Christine read the comments before that. None of them seemed related. It was like the comment dropped out of the blue. She typed in, "Ha ha! I'm right here!" But no one responded. The next day, someone sent a random text about their boss. But that strange comment—"Don't tell Christine"—weighed on her. She fought against her old insecurity, that she wasn't really a core part of the group.

The next week, Beth called her. As it turned out, three years prior, someone had accidentally sent a text to everyone on the text group but Christine. Although it had started as an accident, it had continued as a joke—a parallel ghost text chain, running alongside the one that included Christine. It was meant as harmless, Beth assured her.

After they hung up, Christine didn't know if this information made her feel better. These were old friends, not ones she saw much anymore. Still, it was strange for them to connect via text without her—and referring to her in a joke, of all things!

Over the next week, a few apologies from the gang dribbled in. "Just harmless fun," one said. "It got out of control," said another. Christine typically didn't get involved in drama. Who had time? But she realized her sense of trust had been broken. She talked with her husband, Brian, about it. He said, "That's bizarre. I can see a day or two, after an accident. But they did it for years."

"Yes!" Christine said. "Thank you! I thought I was over-reacting!"

"I'm just glad our life is out here," Brian said, waving his arm majestically around the disaster of a living room, piled with laundry. "And not crammed into the text box of a phone." He leaned down and scooped up their son into his arms. "Yeah, we've got it pretty good."

That night, Christine lay awake, thinking. In some ways, keeping up with college friends was like being suspended in amber—they were all stuck relating to one another as if they were still 19 years old. As she was thinking, she saw her phone glow, and glow again. Probably the infinite text, with more banter and chatter. Maybe she'd drop out of it, maybe not. But Brian was right: Her life was here in the real world. Not in texts. The more she could remind herself of that, the better she felt. She turned off her phone. She wasn't angry at her friends. Well, not really. It's just that the infinite text was a message in a bottle from a different time. With the hurt feelings put in their proper place, she snuggled closer to Brian and fell fast asleep, secure in the life she had made for herself.

Love isn't about what we did yesterday;
it's about what we do today and tomorrow
and the day after.

—GRACE LEE BOGGS

TRY THIS

On a piece of paper, list all the people and activities that are important to you. Try to list up to 100 items. Include a friendship that has brought you pain. Now, look at them all. See that painful friendship in perspective, as only one part of the grand mosaic of your life. Alongside compassion, perspective is an essential quality in forgiveness.

No One Is Defined by Their Worst Moment

In their 20s, Cheryl and Dave worked together at a newspaper and had hit it off. They both worked hard and loved to laugh, especially at the fussy editor, who would splutter with frustration when it got close to deadline. Their co-workers sometimes asked about their relationship, but they'd assure them it was only platonic. "We'd drive each other crazy as a couple," was Cheryl's standard line. "It's better this way."

In their 30s, when they were no longer working at the newspaper, they'd get together for drinks a few times a year. Both were married, and their spouses enjoyed taking part in the old, comfortable friendship with stories from the newsroom. Then, Dave moved away, and they lost touch. Around Cheryl's 48th birthday, she was surprised to see a message from Dave saying that he had moved back to town. He was divorced and wanted to be closer to his parents. Cheryl had gone through a painful divorce herself two years before, so she was glad to catch up with an old friend.

They met at a Mexican restaurant with an outdoor patio. It was like no time had passed. As they caught up with each other, the margaritas kept coming. At closing time, neither one was entirely steady on their feet. As they were heading out to the parking lot, Cheryl said she was going to call a Lyft and leave her car at the restaurant. Dave made what was probably an attempt at a joke, about how old and responsible she was now. As she tried to figure out how to download the app for a Lyft, she felt his hand on her back, sliding down to her skirt. She yanked away. "Dave!" she said. It seemed like he had been leaning in for a kiss. He was embarrassed, mumbled an apology, and staggered off to his car. Cheryl was furious. She had always thought Dave was one of the good guys and she had certainly not given him any reason to think they were anything other than friends.

The next day, she received an email with a heartfelt apology. Dave had been in recovery, and then had fallen away. The prior night's incident was a wake-up call for him, and he'd gone back to an AA meeting that morning. He'd understand if Cheryl didn't want to see him again, but he wanted to apologize.

Cheryl thought about the confident young man she had known, in contrast to this man now in middle age, recently failing to maintain his recovery journey. The two images were so different, but they were the same person. A wave of compassion went through her when she thought of Dave in these terms: as a story with a lot of chapters that was not over yet. Whether or not their friendship continued, she would choose to see him as more than his worst moment.

> Let nothing disturb you. Let nothing frighten
> you. Everything passes away, except God.
> Patience brings everything. Whoever has God
> lacks nothing. God alone is enough.
>
> —ST. TERESA OF AVILA (TRANSLATED BY AUTHOR)

TRY THIS

No one is defined only by their worst moment. As you consider the person you're trying to forgive, think with compassion of the varied chapters of their life—the high points and low points. Think of the struggles the person might face ahead. You do this not to excuse the behavior that hurt you, but to cultivate compassion within you for the whole person. Consider praying that God would bless both of your lives with peace and growing wisdom, despite (or through) the inevitable missteps.

After Loss, Regrowth

Bill and Peter were friends from the local lunchtime Rotary Club. They enjoyed doing service projects together, especially clearing trails. One day in the woods, Peter, who was in business, asked if Bill, a middle-school principal, wanted to invest in a development project. Bill had always been cautious about investing, but, after talking it over with his wife, he took the plunge. From that moment on, the project seemed beset with setbacks. Still, Bill trusted Peter. At least until the day when Peter pulled him aside at a Rotary meeting to let him know his investment was gone. Bill was incredulous. Peter originally said the deal was a "slam dunk." Now, there was a long explanation about sunk costs and contingencies and other things Bill couldn't quite follow.

Bill felt stupid for not asking for more information. It had never occurred to him that all that money could just disappear. He lost an enormous portion of his savings.

Six months later, he saw the building he'd invested in was under construction. The name of Peter's company was out front. Bill had a flicker of hope that the deal had been salvaged. But when asked, Peter said no, this building was funded by other investors. There was no trace of empathy. This was just business. Bill began to have stomachaches from his anger. He and his wife had cut their expenses to try to recoup some of their heavy losses, but it seemed as though Peter was only growing more successful. He had two other buildings going up around town.

Over time, Bill's wife was able to forgive him for losing so much of their money; after all, she said, she had agreed to the deal. But it took Bill longer to forgive Peter, who seemed to have suffered no consequences for playing fast and loose with their savings. Peter seemed to be thriving despite having done someone wrong. Bill wanted to let go of the angst. He wanted to live without the stomachaches from the stress. But that was easier said than done.

One day, he had an idea. He went to the garden store and bought a small tree, which he planted in his backyard. It symbolized returning to his own basic commitments. He was an educator, invested in children. He was an outdoorsman, invested in the enjoyment of nature. This tree represented where he had rooted himself and his life, and the nurture these things required. He went out to check on the tree every day. As it grew, and as Bill focused more and more on what was important to him, the stress and the stomachaches lessened. He'd lost some money, but he was not going to lose what was important to him. He thought about the idea that a storm can strengthen a tree, and that's what he hoped the bad experience would do for his life.

Two years later, when the tree towered over Bill's head, he hadn't forgotten the shock of the financial deal. But he was even more deeply rooted in what was important to him, in his own life. He still went out there almost every day, to remember what it represented: his renewed commitment to what mattered to him.

> *Forgiveness is an act of the will, and the will can function regardless of the temperature of the heart.*
>
> —CORRIE TEN BOOM, AUTHOR

TRY THIS

Think of a symbolic action that would actively engage you in defining your own life. It could even be planting a tree, like Bill did. Once you've found a symbol for your own life's commitments, regularly engage in that symbol. It's a way to return from the anxious focus on the other person and what they did, back to the peaceful focus on yourself and your own goodness.

So much of friendship depends on external conditions and shared experiences: going to the same school, playing on the same team, working in the same department. You can think of your friends in superficial terms, as "classmate," "teammate," or "colleague," instead of seeing them more fully, as the people they are and where they come from. Conflict can arise out of differences or experiences you don't understand. You first learn how to handle tension within your family, and you bring those methods into friendships. Some people distance themselves when tension arises. Others lash out. Others involve a third person in hopes of calming things down. Understandably, you can take these behaviors personally. After all, how your friend responds in conflict feels like a demonstration of their feelings for you.

Practicing compassion, even with one who's hurt you, is like being a movie director and asking the camera to take in a wider view. As the shot pans out, showing more and more of the scene, we can see the object of our attention in greater context. As you widen your view of your friends beyond categories like "classmate" or "neighbor," you begin to see them in a richer context. You see how their behavior might be an expression of their family norms. Or of their cultural norms. You might see how living with a particular marginalized identity has required them to develop certain defensive mechanisms that rise up in moments of tension. You might see how their family dynamics affect their ability to communicate. Holding your friends in this wider view can help you understand, or at least begin to form a hunch about, behavior that otherwise wouldn't make any sense.

YOU EITHER GET BITTER OR YOU GET BETTER. IT'S THAT SIMPLE. YOU EITHER TAKE WHAT HAS BEEN DEALT TO YOU AND ALLOW IT TO MAKE YOU A BETTER PERSON, OR YOU ALLOW IT TO TEAR YOU DOWN. THE CHOICE DOES NOT BELONG TO FATE, IT BELONGS TO YOU.

—JOSH SHIPP, AUTHOR AND YOUTH SPEAKER

CHAPTER 4

COLLEAGUES

In my early 20s, I worked at a deli where 10 people worked together for hours in a space half the size of a school bus. You bet there were times tensions flared. Even something as straightforward as making sandwiches could be fraught with complexity—because it wasn't about the sandwiches. There were relationships with peers, management, and customers to negotiate. Because our income came from our work, things could get really tense.

Sometimes, what's at stake is our sense of meaning and purpose. For some people, a job is only a paycheck, a way to fund meaningful endeavors outside the workplace. When I was making sandwiches, my off-hours making music were more important to me than the deli. But, for many people, a job isn't only how they make money. It's how they make a difference. It's an expression of who they are, and what's important to them. Challenges with colleagues or bosses or subordinates can seem to threaten their ability to express who they are. Talk about high stakes!

There's no way around it: To sustain a work-life balance requires you to sustain relationships, many times with people with whom you would not have chosen to spend so many hours. Like any relationship, those at work will inevitably bring misunderstanding, frustration, or worse. The workplace can be a nexus for stressors like favoritism, competition, unfair bias, or lack of recognition. There are conditions that are out of your control. There's an old line that says, "People don't quit jobs; they quit bosses." Some working conditions or bosses are unworthy of the sacrifice they ask of your integrity, no matter the pay.

As you engage in your work, the quality of your heart will determine a lot. If you cultivate a spirit of forgiveness, compassion, and generosity, you may find the inevitable bumps in the road are encountered with shock absorbers. From the heart of forgiveness comes the capacity to collaborate even with those who've caused friction. Mind you, that's not normal. What's normal is to gossip, to get bitter, or to become resigned. But the journey of Christian faith and the journey of forgiveness was never meant to be normal. As Paul says in his letter to the community in Rome (Romans 12:2), "Do not be conformed to this world, but be transformed by the renewing of your minds, so that you may discern what is the will of God—what is good and acceptable and perfect."

Whatever your job, keep Paul's words in mind when you show up at your workplace. Instead of conforming to the cutthroat and shame-inducing values all around, what if you were transformed by the renewing of your mind, so that you showed up in the workplace as a vehicle of God's all-redeeming love? What if your vocation wasn't only the completion of projects and tasks, but the transformation of relationships in your workplace? That's the challenge and invitation in the reflections that follow in this chapter.

Sticking with God When Others Don't Stick with You

Sally was always bailing her boss, Missy, out of one jam or another: inventory control, computer updating, you name it. Sally was there to make it right. But when the department got dinged by a corporate audit, Missy got chewed out and came back with the announcement that no one would be getting a raise that year. They'd all need to undergo retraining. For a month, Sally had been after Missy to submit a recommendation for the professional development that would put Sally on a management track. But now Missy said that no one from their department was going to get any special perks until things got straightened out. Sally couldn't believe it. After all she'd done to bail Missy out, only to get thrown under the bus! Sally had imagined a long history at the company; she'd hoped to rise through the ranks. But now she was blocked. And she didn't want to start over at a new company. All she could think to do was to stew in her sense of betrayal.

Sally had always been curious about the Bible and had been taking an online course about the Apostle Paul. He was a complicated character. Sally was drawn to the theme of grace, and she decided that's how she wanted to live. She didn't want to be trapped in this cycle of bitterness toward Missy. One night, the course talked about the Second Letter to Timothy in which Paul is hauled before a judge and looks around to find that his friends have deserted him. It felt just like how Missy had let her hang out to dry with management. But Paul doesn't get mad. He says, "But the Lord stood by me and gave me strength." Even when he's in an actual prison, Paul understands himself as a "Prisoner of Christ." In other words, no matter what life throws at him, he keeps on anchoring himself in a relationship with God.

Sally had only studied the Bible out of curiosity. But now she began to see that it could help her manage her anger toward Missy. She could now see herself not as captive to Missy's shenanigans, but as captive at each turn to God's love. Just as He was with Paul, God was there, standing by her, giving her strength.

At my first defense no one came to my support, but all deserted me. May it not be counted against them! But the Lord stood by me and gave me strength, so that through me the message might be fully proclaimed... So I was rescued from the lion's mouth.

2 TIMOTHY 4:16-17

CONSIDER THIS

Think of Paul's gracious spirit in his moment of betrayal. Maybe you also feel betrayed. To use his words: If "the Lord stood by [you] and gave [you] strength, so that through [you] the message might be fully proclaimed" in your time of hurt and betrayal, what would that look like? Specifically, what would God standing by you look like? With that strength through God's presence, what message would be proclaimed in your life? Would it be "calm in the storm" or "courage when it counts"? If you let your life speak in a way that shows God is at your side, what would people hear?

Bringing Forth What's Within You

Mariela had only been on the intensive care unit nursing staff for a month and already had a problem. Her name was Casey. Casey moved a mile a minute. She couldn't sit still. Maybe she was hazing Mariela, or maybe she was just mean, but Casey couldn't seem to pass by Mariela without making some sort of comment under her breath. It was never a big scene or a showdown. It was just a constant *drip-drip-drip* of negative feedback. About Mariela's hair. About her notes. About how she moved. "Pick it up there a little," Casey would say, hustling past.

Once, she heard Casey sneer something about "Mexicans and drug-dealers." Mariela was the only Latina—in fact, the only person of color—on the nursing staff and got the impression that Casey's bad attitude came from some racist views. Mariela didn't want to make trouble or get a reputation, but Casey's behavior was stressing her out. It was like a weird private power game that Mariela was losing.

On breaks, Mariela was reading a book about the Gospel of Thomas. It wasn't in the Bible. It was a collection of Jesus's sayings that somebody wrote down in the first or second century and was only discovered in Egypt in 1945. Mariela loved what she was reading. For instance, in the Gospel of Thomas, Jesus says, "If those who lead you say to you, 'look, the Kingdom is in the sky,' then the birds will get there first. If they say 'it's in the ocean,' then the fish will get there first. But the Kingdom of God is within you and outside of you. Once you come to know yourselves, you will become known. And you will know that it is you who are the children of the living father." Mariela decided she wasn't going to stew on this any longer. She wasn't going to file a complaint. She wasn't going to wish it away. She was going to act like a child of God.

The next night, she ran into Casey in the parking lot. Mariela said, "Look, I don't know what I did to turn you against me. But I know it's not good for me to resent you or worry about what you'll say next. So

I just wanted to let you know that whatever you say, I'm going to be praying for you and doing my best to love you. Because I'm trying to be a sanctuary for God." She paused, then added, "I just wanted you to know that." For once, Casey was dumbstruck. And, walking away, Mariela felt herself released from the weight she'd been carrying around. No matter what Casey said or did after that, none of it would touch Mariela. She was free.

> *If you bring forth what is within you, what you bring forth will save you. If you do not bring forth what is within you, what you do not bring forth will destroy you.*
>
> THE GOSPEL OF THOMAS, SAYING 70

TRY THIS

Forgiveness (on one's own) isn't reconciliation (between two people). But sometimes peace can come from the power of expressing yourself clearly, with strength and love, to the one who hurt you. It might be in person. It might be in a letter. If you were going to be clear, with strength and love, in your situation, what is it you'd say to someone who hurt you? Try writing it out in a letter addressed to them. You don't need to send it; write it out for yourself.

Coming Back to Your Senses

The guys at the dealership knew how to wind Danny up. He'd always been a fighter. You have to be a fighter if you're as short and scrawny as he is. And the salesmen especially seemed to take delight in that. Danny worked in the garage connected with the dealership, and whenever he brought in keys or needed to run into the showroom, the comments would start. Nothing seemed off limits. His love life: "Got a date this weekend, Danny?" His height: "Danny, can you reach up and get that binder down for me?" And the cackling started soon afterward. Danny would angrily storm off. "Just messing with you, man," they'd say. His temper had lost him more than one job, so he was trying to keep it together. But the guys wouldn't let up.

Danny wanted peaceful, to let go of all those remarks in the showroom, to cultivate a forgiving heart. He didn't want to be so angry anymore. But it wasn't as easy as pasting on a fake smile.

One day at his doctor's office, he found a magazine that talked about an exercise in which you focus on your five senses when you're upset. Like if you're blinded with rage or overwhelmed with sadness. You'd do an inventory of your senses at that exact moment. Such as, "What is it I'm looking at with my eyes right now?" Then, "What sounds am I hearing with my ears right now?" And so on, with touch, smell, and taste. The article said it was a way to shake loose from the grip of overwhelming emotion instead of stewing on what was going on. Danny tried that for a while. To his surprise, it worked.

Then, he began to experiment with it. He'd read about the Apostle Paul in prison, literally in chains, writing this letter to the people in Philippi, encouraging them to be joyful, no matter what. When he started getting hot under the collar, he began to check in on his heart and emotions. What was he feeling? What thoughts were making him feel like that? It was like he'd discovered a superpower! Not only could he become aware of what was happening in him—he could make some decisions about how to react to it.

A few months later, he realized that the salesmen were no longer trying to wind him up. In fact, a couple of them had asked respectful questions about a few of the cars in the garage. Danny was still the same height, but now when he came into the dealership, he was walking tall.

Only, live your life in a manner worthy of the gospel of Christ, so that, whether I come and see you or am absent and hear about you, I will know that you are standing firm in one spirit, striving side by side with one mind for the faith of the gospel, and are in no way intimidated by your opponents. For them this is evidence of their destruction, but of your salvation. And this is God's doing.

PHILIPPIANS 1:27-28

TRY THIS

Finding language for your experience is the bridge between feeling and thinking. Research has shown that labeling your emotional experience has a calming effect. When you are calmer, instead of reacting with fight or flight, you can choose how to respond. Or, as some therapists say, "If you can name it, you can tame it." Try, like Danny did, to notice and name the quality of your emotion.

If You Can Turn It Up, You Can Turn It Down

Kathleen worked up front at an LGBTQIA youth counseling center, handling whatever intense situations came up. What she couldn't handle was the messy breakroom, especially the coffee cups left in the sink. She had posted notes. Mentioned it in staff meetings. One day, when she saw a coffee mug in the breakroom sink that said, "JACK," something snapped. She grabbed the mug, went straight to Jack's office, and slammed it down on his desk so hard that the handle broke off.

Priscilla, the center director, called Kathleen into her office. Kathleen wasn't surprised. Ever since she could remember, her temper had gotten her in trouble. Before Priscilla could say anything, Kathleen muttered, "I'm sorry. Lost my temper. Won't happen again."

"I don't know," said Priscilla. "If I'd seen that coffee cup there, I wouldn't have just broken the handle." Kathleen looked up, surprised. Priscilla went on, "I'd have smashed the whole thing." This was not the conversation that Kathleen expected.

"When I was your age," Priscilla said, "I got angry a lot, too. It would just come over me. Like being possessed. Like there was nothing I could do." Kathleen nodded. Priscilla understood her. "But the truth is," Priscilla continued, "It also worked for me. It got me what I wanted. And it kept people out of my business. People were always walking on eggshells around me. Losing your temper can be a great strategy."

Kathleen was surprised. She said, "But it's not a strategy. It just happens. I just lose control."

Priscilla smiled. "That's what I used to think, too. People were always telling me to get it together, to calm myself down." Kathleen nodded. That sounded familiar. "I never knew how to do that," Priscilla said. "But then somebody taught me that, if I can turn it up, I can turn it down."

She began writing on a piece of paper. It was a personnel document, a disciplinary form. She handed it to Kathleen. In the box labeled, "Problem Observed," it said, "Not angry enough." Under "Recommended Course of Action," Priscilla had written, "Must express anger more vigorously. Will start with plate smashing."

Kathleen looked up. Priscilla was smiling.

The next day, Kathleen met Priscilla out back of the building, at the loading dock, part of which overlooked the dumpster. In two neat stacks were some chipped dishes. "Got 'em from Goodwill," said Priscilla, proudly. For the next 20 minutes, Kathleen smashed every last one of those old plates in the dumpster, with Priscilla shouting, "Harder!" and "Make it count!" By the end, they were both laughing.

Priscilla said, "For a long time, I tried to rein in my temper. To bite my tongue. To clamp down how I felt. And I still felt out of control. When somebody told me, 'If you can turn it up, you can turn it down,' it seemed backward. But it worked. If I could yell louder? If I could make myself angrier? It didn't make sense. Then I realized I had some control and choice over how I was acting. If I could turn it up, I *could* turn it down."

Kathleen nodded without saying a word. This was all new information. But it was a relief to hear she didn't have to be captive to her anger anymore. She had choices. She could be even angrier, if she wanted. Or, who knows, maybe she'd decide she didn't want to be angry anymore. All she knew was that it was up to her.

Bear with each other and forgive one
another if any of you has a grievance against
someone. Forgive as the Lord forgave you.

COLOSSIANS 3:13

TRY THIS

On your forgiveness journey, if you've been overly expressive to the point where you're trying to rein in or hold back emotions or thoughts, try the opposite. Amplify them. See if you can "turn it up." Once you realize you have choices, you can decide which choice you would like to make. Like Kathleen's smashing of chipped plates in a dumpster, make sure your own exercises are done in a safe way. This exercise isn't prescribed for everyone. If you've ever been fired for your temper, been accused (or found guilty) of abusive behavior, only consider this exercise in consultation with a therapist. Since expressing strong feelings are bound to be exhausting, have a self-soothing plan for afterward (like drinking a cup of hot tea or listening to calming music).

Help Yourself

Every day, 10 minutes before opening, the Good Food grocery staff started the day with a Team Huddle. Everybody on shift crowded around as the manager on duty gave a little pep talk. Sometimes he handed out gift cards to recognize special effort. It was supposed to lift morale, but it had the opposite effect on Sean. Not once had a manager recognized him. It wasn't really about the gift card. It was about somebody noticing how hard he had worked.

Sean worked in the produce department, and it meant not only heavy lifting and straining to reach into the bins, it took knowing how to tell with a glance when an item was getting past its prime. It wasn't going to save the world. It was just a job. But he took it seriously. He didn't slack off. And no one seemed to notice.

One day, he was out back on a smoke break with the one of the managers, Jeff. Sean asked, "Hey man, what does somebody have to do to get noticed around here?"

Jeff gave him a look. "What do you mean?"

Sean explained how he felt about the Team Huddles and never getting a gift card. Jeff's brow furrowed with care. He was really listening. He said some kind things about Sean's work. But then the next Team Huddle came. And the next. A month went by. Sean had poured out his heart to Jeff. And it was like Jeff had just forgotten.

One day, after stocking a mountain of cabbages perfectly, Sean said in a wise-guy voice, "Great job, Sean."

"Talking to yourself?" somebody called from the next aisle.

Even though he'd meant it sarcastically, it gave Sean an idea. He began to notice when he'd done a good job, and he'd pause to recognize it—without the sarcasm. After a while of giving himself the recognition he hadn't received from others, he noticed other people who he appreciated, too. He began to make comments like, "Nice display up there, Carlos." "The bulk section's looking tight, Bree."

It was like he was showing up in a different store. He didn't care about the Team Huddles anymore. He didn't need them to judge his performance or give him a party. He was realizing he could have his own party everywhere he went. Years later, when people would ask how he came to develop such a warm, loving heart, he'd tell them how feeling put-out had led to a daily—really, hourly—gratitude practice.

> *Hate has caused a lot of problems in this world, but it has not solved one yet.*
>
> —MAYA ANGELOU

CONSIDER THIS

The Catholic mystic Thomas Merton said, "To be grateful is to recognize the Love of God in everything He has given us—and He has given us everything. Every breath we draw is a gift of His love. . . . Gratitude therefore takes nothing for granted, is never unresponsive, is constantly awakening to new wonder and to praise of the goodness of God." Even when nothing about your situation changes or resolves, start a tenacious gratitude practice. Open your heart to see what beauty and goodness you've been overlooking. Give thanks for everything you encounter. See what happens.

AS YOUR MEDITATION BECOMES
DEEPER IT WILL DEFEND YOU
FROM THE PERPETUAL ASSAULTS
OF THE OUTER WORLD. YOU WILL
HEAR THE BUSY HUM OF THAT
WORLD AS A DISTANT EXTERIOR
MELODY AND KNOW YOURSELF TO
BE IN SOME SORT WITHDRAWN
FROM IT. YOU HAVE SET A RING OF
SILENCE BETWEEN YOU AND IT;
AND BEHOLD! WITHIN THAT
SILENCE YOU ARE FREE.

—EVELYN UNDERHILL

Welcoming Everyone Home

Three months ago, Dan had been invited to a board meeting at church. He'd worked at First Christian for six years, as Associate Minister, but had never been to a board meeting before. His specialty was pastoral care—listening to people and loving them, warts and all. As he entered the boardroom, everyone looked at him. He sat. Immediately, the Senior Minister began to tear into him. She listed all his administrative and organizational shortcomings without any mention of the many hospital visits and caring phone calls he'd made—not a word about the pastoral work that was his true calling. It was an ambush. Out of the blue, he'd been fired. In front of everyone.

Worse: No one in the room had risen to his defense. Not Jeff, who Dan had tended to throughout his divorce. Or Beth Ann, whom he'd comforted after her mother had died. Church members he had supported did nothing. Although he soon picked up work as a hospital chaplain, he couldn't stop replaying that night in his head. There were countless ways it could have gone gracefully. Instead, it was a public humiliation.

But one morning, while reflecting on the story of the Prodigal Son, something shifted in Dan. For months, wounded by the experience, he had seen himself as a victim, helpless in response. He felt as if he were the wayward Prodigal Son, waiting to be welcomed home. He was waiting to be forgiven for his failings. As he reflected, he realized he could identify with other characters in the same story: the forgiving father, the jealous brother, the servants. He began to imagine himself from those angles.

What if it was his old boss and the church members who had strayed and it was up to him to play the role of the generous father, extending forgiveness? What if he was the jealous brother, keeping score and withholding forgiveness for flawed humans—the senior minister and church members—when God's love stood ready to welcome *them* home, warts and all? He had spent so many hours ruminating on the experience, and the mistreatment *he* suffered. Now he began to explore the complex dimensions of what happened with all the people involved. He began to see the Senior Minister as someone trapped in a difficult situation. He saw church members timid, unable to stand up for what was right. He didn't condone their behavior. He still had healing to do. But identifying with different characters in the story helped him escape the rut he'd been in. His journey of compassion and forgiveness had begun.

> *You have heard that it was said, 'You shall love your neighbor and hate your enemy.' But I say to you, 'Love your enemies and pray for those who persecute you. . . .'*
> THE GOSPEL OF MATTHEW 5:43-44

TRY THIS

Consider your experience in light of the Parable of the Prodigal Son (found in the Gospel of Luke [15:11-32]). Take the perspective of the wayward son as you think of your own experience and betrayal: What is he feeling? What does he need? What does he fear? What does he see? What does he want? Now, one by one, take the perspectives of other characters in the story, such as the father and the elder brother. In each, using the same questions, reflect on your own experience as if through their eyes.

Discovering Clearness

If she needed to work twice as hard to get half the credit, Rachael was going to work four times as hard. She felt that was part of being a Black woman in this world. This past week the marketing firm she worked for had a shot at the Hank's Steaks account. Landing it would be huge for her firm. Her boss knew Rachael could handle a challenge, so he put her on the project. Unfortunately, he paired her with Todd Stimson.

Todd showed up to meetings unprepared, but made people laugh so they let him off the hook. As Rachael worked day and night on the Hank's Steaks presentation, with the central concept of "sizzle," Todd dropped off the radar. But at least *she* was prepared. She arrived at the Hank's Steaks headquarters 30 minutes early and took a seat. She was reviewing her notes when she heard laughter. Todd and Hank Ballard himself entered the waiting area, as if they were old friends. "Rachael," Todd cried in mock horror. "We almost let Hank here go with the 'sizzle' concept! I told him we can do better. Come on! Let's do some spit-balling and see if we can't do a whole lot better for him!" Todd and Hank disappeared into the conference room.

Rachael had known plenty of Todds in her life. But now there was a volcano inside her. It was all she could do to hold back tears of rage.

That night, her best friend, Diane, came over. "Seems like you got punished for following the rules and other people got rewarded for just winging it," Diane summarized. When Rachael started talking about quitting her job, Diane held up her hand. "Hold up," she said. "Let's not take drastic measures. I've got an idea." Diane had attended a Quaker college and learned some Quaker traditions. One was to gather a "Clearness Committee."

A week later, Diane and three other people close to Rachael gathered in her apartment. They had a brief time of prayer together. Then, they listened to Rachael's questions and concerns. She'd been carrying anger inside her for a long time—for Todd and for the people who enabled Todd and all the other slackers—and she wanted to release it. She just didn't know how. Her friends listened patiently. Then, allowing for silences, they began to ask their own, open-ended questions. They reflected some of what they'd heard. They discussed Rachael's own guiding principles, her hopes for relating to others at work, and her understanding of God's place in her anger and in her healing from anger.

None of this changed the unfair conditions at work. But, from that night on, Rachael had a lighter heart and a clearer mind about how she would relate to it all. Her tenacity would not be born of anger. It would be born of faith.

Because of the favor of God, we can have peace in the midst of chaos.

—CRYSTAL McDOWELL

TRY THIS

Gather a few trusted souls as a Clearness Committee to support you in engaging your relationship to a difficult situation. Make sure everyone understands some simple guidelines for the conversation: cultivate a spirit of prayer, do not give advice (only ask open-ended questions that can't be answered with a simple yes or no), and allow plenty of quiet time for reflection.

The Mood or the Mission?

The Stone Soup Food Bank was an inspiring success. In only 10 years, it had grown from an idea into a warehouse that provided nonperishable items—from canned goods to diapers—to tens of thousands of people each week.

Although a lot of his time was spent fundraising, co-founder Barry still liked to volunteer in the warehouse, working shoulder to shoulder with others in the Stone Soup community. He was grateful for the other co-founder, Paul. Paul did what Barry called "all the boring stuff." Even once the organization grew so large, Paul insisted on doing the bookkeeping himself. Everyone was impressed with Paul's commitment to detail.

But when the treasurer pulled Barry aside one night, saying that some of Paul's numbers didn't add up, Barry wasn't totally surprised. He'd wondered about the finances at Stone Soup. Even with large donations, Stone Soup only ever seemed to break even. An audit revealed that Paul had been skimming from the organization for years. He eventually went to prison.

The Board reluctantly asked Barry to resign. As much as people loved him, as co-founder Barry should have done a better job of protecting people's gifts. The Board needed to save Stone Soup and to rebuild trust throughout the community. Barry had to go.

Barry spent almost six months in a funk. How could he trust anyone, if even stout-hearted Paul had been revealed to be a thief? Barry's wife asked if he would ever visit Paul in prison, but Barry couldn't imagine bringing himself to do that. He was just too broken-hearted. One day, his wife said, "How long are you going to serve yourself and not others?" She said she knew he was hurting. But he needed to decide what he would put first: his mood or his mission. That kindled something in Barry. Even as he continued to nurse the hurt of broken trust, and even some cynicism that had leaked in, he began to spend time in prayer and reflection, trying to discern what he was called to do now.

He realized what he'd been through was part of his mission. God wanted him to walk alongside people who had experienced broken trust on both sides: victims and perpetrators of crimes. He even visited Paul to tell him about it. It would take a long time for Barry to trust other people again. But he would no longer let his mood come before his mission.

The most authentic thing about us is our
capacity to create, to overcome, to endure,
to transform, to love and to be greater
than our suffering.

—BEN OKRI

CONSIDER THIS

1.   Has injury from a colleague or boss ever stopped you from doing or being something important?

2.   Is it possible to view growth from that injury as having a greater positive impact in the world than the negative impact you experienced?

Not Serving Two Masters

The math department at Douglass Middle School was composed of only six people, and five of them had worked together now for more than 10 years. John and Carl had taught there the longest, each almost 20 years. John loved his work, but he had never much enjoyed being colleagues with Carl McAffee. Carl was also the boys' basketball coach, and he brought that intensity into both the classroom and collegial relations. It was especially a problem every spring during the annual standardized testing required of every student in school. Within hours of the scores being sent to the teachers, Carl would casually show up in the doorway of his classroom. "So," Carl would say, "how'd they do?"

John was never too invested in test preparation. He saw his class as a foundation of mathematical understanding on which the students would continue to build over the years ahead. But Carl spent the year focused on getting his students ready for the test. He ran practice tests, drill sessions, and sent information home to the parents about test-taking strategies. Inevitably, Carl's students got higher scores than John's students. John could live with that. But Carl's smugness ate at him. Even when John explained that he was after long-term effects in the kids' understanding, Carl would listen with a smirk. As if to say, "Yeah, right, loser." Carl liked to post rankings of the various classes' scores in the hallway. Supposedly, it was to celebrate the kids. John felt it was really to declare victory for Carl himself, once again.

At a Memorial Day picnic one year, John's daughter, Claire, asked him, "Why do you let him steal your joy and take up space in your head like that?" Claire was 14 years old. John didn't know where she'd learned such insight. "Last year, when those girls were bullying me, you told me what Jesus said, that people can't serve two masters. You said I could decide if I was going to let those girls and their opinions be my master, or if I was going to decide in my heart to follow God." She paused. "Well, it just seems you're letting Mr. McAffee be your master, and not God."

John chuckled. "I'm going to need to spend some time thinking about that. But I have to say, Claire, I'm impressed. That's some wise stuff."

"Well," she said, grabbing another potato chip, "I learned from the best."

> *No one can serve two masters; for a slave will either hate the one and love the other, or be devoted to the one and despise the other. You cannot serve God and wealth.*
>
> MATTHEW 6:24

CONSIDER THIS

1. Have you allowed the person who hurt you to have a more powerful influence on you than God?

2. In your journey of forgiveness, if you were more focused on God and less focused on the other person, what would that look like? What would change?

Remembering What You Want

Esme loved the Army Reserves. The discipline. The friendships. The sense of purpose. She loved the drill weekends when everybody arrived, fired up and ready for the training and exercises they had planned. Her enthusiasm got noticed. Three months ago, her company commander put her in charge of a platoon. The platoon was full of her friends, and they still wanted to joke around like they always had. But she had to back off a little bit. She was their leader now. They teased her about it, but generally understood. Then came the scandal.

The recent fitness scores seemed a little fishy—too many people had scored too high on push-ups and sit-ups. On investigation, it turned out that a few Sergeants, not wanting the soldiers to get punished for falling below the standard, had written down inflated numbers. The company's Commander ensured it was being handled, but he wanted Esme to know a few of the culprits were in her platoon.

She was furious. How could they?! It was against everything that the Army stood for. The next week, when she and the Commander talked again, she told him how angry she was, how she couldn't stop thinking about it.

He said, "If you had a magic wand, and everything in the platoon would be the way you want it to be, what would that look like?"

"Well, sir," she said, "no one would have cheated."

"Okay," he said. "But we can't change the past. So with things as they are, what would you say? What do you want to be true in the platoon?"

Esme said, without pausing, "Sir, I want people to be fired up. I want them to work together and support one another to do hard things they think they can't do. I want them to stay honorable and act with dignity, Sir, especially when they're in uniform."

"Well then, Lieutenant," he said, "it sounds like you've got a vision for your platoon. And what's your part in it?"

"Sir, I've got to step up and lead them to want those things," she said, "And to work for them, too. Some of them weren't raised like I was. I've got to develop them."

Esme had been so focused on her anger and disappointment. But when her Commander asked the magic wand question, she started to get clear on what it was that she wanted—for the platoon and from herself. Reoriented now to what she wanted in the future, instead of what she couldn't change in the past, the anger and disappointment subsided a bit. She began to plan for the next time she'd see her soldiers, and what it would look like to lead them to be what she knew they could be.

> If you want to identify me, ask me not where I live, or what I like to eat, or how I comb my hair, but ask me what I think I am living for, in detail, ask me what I think is keeping me from living fully for the thing I want to live for.
>
> –THOMAS MERTON

CONSIDER THIS

One technique of Solution-Focused Brief Therapy is called the "Miracle Question," which is similar to what the Commander asked in the story. See if you can apply it to your situation: *"Suppose you woke up one morning and by some miracle everything you ever wanted, everything good you could ever imagine for yourself, had actually happened—your life had turned out exactly the way you wanted it...."*

1. What will you notice around you that let you know that the miracle had happened?

2. What will you see?

3. What will you hear?

4. What will you feel inside yourself?

5. How will you be different?

With a vivid understanding of your own goals, you can start to choose your behavior, no longer hamstrung by that of others. What choices will you make today?

Business consultant Peter Drucker is known to have said, "Culture eats strategy for breakfast." A company can have the most ambitious strategies and powerful operational systems, but the determining variable in its success is its culture. You may not be able to drive high-level strategy or to change policies. But anyone, at any position, can lead culture change. If your workplace has become dehumanized—that is, people and their efforts aren't recognized and appreciated—you can start to reverse that today. You can be an agent of "rehumanization." See if you can learn people's stories: What makes them tick? What gets them up in the morning? What do they care about? What do they fear? Heck, what are their favorite movies? It doesn't need to start with something deep. What you're doing is helping create a workplace culture in which people relate to one another as something other than cogs in a machine. This will take time. It will take the commitment of time to be present for your colleagues—to listen to them tell you about their dog, even if you don't especially care about dogs. It will also take time in another sense: Culture change isn't an overnight thing. It asks for your long-haul commitment. A workplace culture in which the roots of compassion are nourished and allowed to take hold will be the kind of culture that promotes and encourages the habit of forgiveness.

**FORGIVENESS AND COMPASSION
ARE ALWAYS LINKED: HOW DO
WE HOLD PEOPLE ACCOUNTABLE
FOR WRONGDOING AND YET AT
THE SAME TIME REMAIN IN TOUCH
WITH THEIR HUMANITY ENOUGH TO
BELIEVE IN THEIR CAPACITY
TO BE TRANSFORMED?**

—bell hooks, AUTHOR AND ACTIVIST

CHAPTER 5

COMMUNITY

In the late 1980s, the sociologist Ray Oldenburg argued for the importance of "third places" in society. If the first place a person spends their life is at home and the second place is at work, a "third place" is out in the world—congregations, cafes, clubs, pubs, and corner stores—places where people encounter one another and form community. Oldenburg said these places were important for fostering the kind of civic relations and understanding that sustains civil society. But in the year 2000, another sociologist, Robert Putnam, published the book called *Bowling Alone*, which reported the fraying of these kinds of relationships and community experiences.

Whether practicing faith in a congregation, fulfilling a sense of service through volunteering, or pursuing an avocation like singing in a community chorus, being part of community is important to democracy and society, just as Ray Oldenburg said. It also brings richness and purpose to life, to feel part of something larger. The relationships made in community are precious. They can also be messy.

You can fall out with a neighbor. You can get tense with someone at church. Someone in your book group can hurt your feelings, to the point where you're not sure if you want to go back. When those relationships fray, you can understand why Robert Putnam observed the steady erosion of community life in this country. Maybe it's easier to just stay at home, to not risk getting hurt. But even as you consider withdrawing, and hiding out back at home, you know how much these "third places" have meant to you.

The Christian faith, by and large, is not intended as a solitary practice. "Wherever two or three are gathered in my name," Jesus says, in the Gospel of Matthew 18:20, "I am there among them." By faith, and evolutionarily, you are wired for life in community. You aren't meant to go it alone.

So if you're going to stick it out, if you're going to commit to life in community, you're going to need to learn to practice forgiveness. The people we'll meet out there in the world are imperfect. And so are we.

Meeting in the Field of Suffering

Hackett Lane was a quiet cul-de-sac where three cats could lie in the middle of the road all afternoon without stirring. Emily had lived there for 30 years now. She had considered moving after David died, but was glad she had stayed. Her cats Squiggy, Dale, and Moe kept her company. It was a peaceful life until Mr. Duncan, who lived across the street, got sick. She was glad he could get home health aid, but the healthcare assistants who drove in and out of Hackett Lane put her cats at risk. There was one young woman in a blue Toyota who drove into the cul-de-sac with particular recklessness. Emily put up a sign that said, "PLEASE DRIVE SLOWLY—CATS." But to no avail. Without warning, the blue Toyota would careen around the corner and bomb down the street to Mr. Duncan's house. One day, when it happened again, Emily strode across the street.

"Excuse me," she said. The young woman turned around. Emily explained about the cats lying in the street and the need to drive slowly. She might as well have been speaking an alien language for all the reaction she got. Not one week later, a neighbor rang her bell. One of her cats had been killed. Squiggy. It wasn't fair! Losing David had been enough. How was she supposed to now absorb another loss?

When the young woman emerged from Mr. Duncan's house, Emily practically leaped through the doorway and flew across the street. She laid into the young woman, calling into question her parents and background and general character.

The young woman burst into tears. "I'm so sorry," she said. "I've been so worried about Mr. Duncan. It's my first job, and … he's so sweet. He sang me a song my grandfather used to sing, and … he's going to die, I think." She wiped her nose with the back of her hand. "I'm so sorry about your cat."

A week later, at Mr. Duncan's funeral, Emily saw the young woman in tears, sitting in the back row. She went and sat beside her. And took her hand. There was not much to say. They didn't have much in common. But suffering of any kind, including grief, invites a certain communion beyond any words. Emily still thought this young woman was reckless and had a lot of growing up to do. But she decided that she would choose sharing grief in a spirit of forgiveness rather than holding a grudge. It was, in the end, the only way to move forward.

To love means loving the unlovable. To forgive means pardoning the unpardonable. Faith means believing the unbelievable. Hope means hoping when everything seems hopeless.

—G. K. CHESTERTON, AUTHOR AND PHILOSOPHER

TRY THIS

We are, naturally, more aware of our own suffering than the suffering of others. As you think about the person who hurt you, see if you can understand the nature of their own suffering. Pray for them, that their suffering might be eased. Pray for yourself, asking God to release you from the duty of judgment.

Building a House for Forgiveness

Over the years, many volunteers have spent hours in the sun building Habitat for Humanity projects. Gordie and Bill had been meeting up at project sites now for more than 10 years. They respected each other's carpentry skills and would exchange small talk on a water break. Otherwise, it was all work.

One Saturday, Gordie and Bill were working on a duplex. Both of the soon-to-be homeowners were there, contributing their "sweat equity." The project was moving along. Gordie was up on the roof, securing flashing to the edge of the chimney when he heard shouting. It was Bill. "No, no, no!" Bill was shouting, as if Gordie was a child or a dog. "That's not the flashing they wanted. You got it out of the wrong pile!" Gordie had noticed that Bill liked to fancy himself as a person who stood up for the homeowners. But this was too far, getting shouted at. When Gordie asked, "Why don't you calm down?" Bill replied, "Why don't you learn to check your work?"

Among people like Bill and Gordie, these were fighting words. "Measure twice, cut once" was a principle they lived by. To suggest that someone had been careless or less than deliberate in their approach was the highest insult. Bill walked away in a huff. Gordie stayed on the roof and continued to secure the flashing. He knew he hadn't made a mistake; Bill was wrong. But it ticked Gordie off to be called out like that, as if was his first Saturday on the site.

At lunch break, he found he could hardly look over at where Bill was sitting with his sandwich. Gordie had been married to Jean for many years by that point, and he'd learned a lot about forgiveness from their relationship. One thing the couple had figured out a long time ago is that it's hard to stay mad at someone if you're cooperating on something. With Jean, it was often cooking dinner together. If they were in the kitchen, passing ingredients and helping each other, something shifted. Now, out on the worksite, Gordie thought he'd try something like that with Bill. He walked over and proposed that they put in the stairs together. Doing stairs wasn't like banging a nail into drywall. You really had to get the measurements right so things didn't turn out wonky. Bill looked at him a moment and then agreed.

For the rest of the afternoon, Bill and Gordie worked side by side on the front staircase, all the way to the final touch: an elegant newel post at the bottom of the railing, complete with a hand-carved wooden knob at the top. When the sun was going down and it was time to quit, Bill said gruffly as he was walking off, "Good working together today." Gordie replied, "Same here. See you next week." Working together had helped them both forgive.

Forgiveness is the name of love practiced among people who love poorly. The hard truth is that all people love poorly. We need to forgive and be forgiven every day, every hour increasingly. That is the great work of love among the fellowship of the weak that is the human family.

–HENRI J. M. NOUWEN, CATHOLIC PRIEST AND AUTHOR

TRY THIS

At first, finding a common project or task or mission with the one who has hurt you may seem undesirable. After all, you may want to just avoid them! But, on the journey of forgiveness, engaging in a shared project, especially in service of a larger purpose, can create or reinforce a broader view of the relationship than merely that of the recent conflict. If it seems right for you, give it a try.

Meeting Hatred with Love

In the late 1980s, one of the best high school girls' basketball players in the state of South Dakota was SuAnne Big Crow. She played for the Lady Thorpes, from the high school on the Pine Ridge Reservation, home to the Oglala Sioux. SuAnne wasn't only a talented basketball player. She was also a leader with a generous heart. Her dream was to go to college so she could come back to the reservation and be a resource to her people, especially the kids.

Late in the 1989 season, the Lady Thorpes traveled to play a game in the city of Lead, South Dakota. That night, the gymnasium was full of rowdy fans, many shouting racist taunts at the visiting Indigenous team. A few of the Lady Thorpe players were afraid to go out on the court in front of such hostility. But SuAnne walked out of the locker room and to center court. She took off her warm-up jacket and draped it on her shoulders. She began to perform the traditional shawl dance with her jacket and started singing in Lakota.

The crowd grew quieter. Where there had been mockery, now there was respect. In the Civil Rights era, the Rev. Dr. Martin Luther King Jr. cautioned, "Let no man pull you so low that you hate him." SuAnne Big Crow refused to hate the basketball fans in Lead. Instead, she responded with generosity and dignity.

Tragically, SuAnne Big Crow died in a car accident in 1992, when she was a high school senior. But the legacy of her short life lives on. A teammate reported that the girls' basketball teams from Pine Ridge and from Lead became friendly after SuAnne's shawl dance. And her dreams of helping the kids at Pine Ridge were realized when the SuAnne Big Crow Boys and Girls Club was established in her honor. Every year now, the National Education Association recognizes the student who has most contributed to other students' sense of worth and dignity. It's called the SuAnne Big Crow Award. Many still remember her kindness and her leadership. And many still tell the story of when she responded to racialized hatred with the power and beauty of the culture and tradition she loved.

Forgiveness means it finally becomes unimportant that you hit back.

—ANNE LAMOTT, BEST-SELLING AUTHOR

CONSIDER THIS

1. If you were on the receiving end of hatred and disrespect from a group, as was the Pine Ridge girls' basketball team, how would you want to respond? What quality of heart and what actions would convey what you stood for? How would you need to prepare to respond in that moment?

2. As you think about your current situation in your journey of forgiveness, what do you need to do to engage it in the way you intend?

Keeping Eyes on the Prize

Joe lived in a small city near a larger city. In his small city, some congregations joined to act as the voice of faith on issues related to racism in housing and the rights of immigrants. In the larger city nearby, other people of faith were doing the same thing. Grant money was available to both groups if they banded together. They decided to join forces. From the start, things were rocky. There was jealousy about how much time the community organizer was spending in one city versus the other. There were differing opinions about how to make decisions. The members of the group from the larger city had the habit of lecturing Joe and others as if they were the experts. They decided to part ways.

The group from the larger city announced that they would be keeping the entire amount of money from the grant. Joe had kept his cool through the patronizing lectures and through the tiresome bickering about decision-making processes. But for this organization to unilaterally decide to keep tens of thousands of dollars seemed not only unethical, it seemed illegal. After all the time he and his congregation had poured into it, trying to broker a partnership in the name of justice, it just wasn't fair! These were supposed to be people of faith. Now, the group in his small city had become demoralized and was falling apart.

On a walk by the river, Joe began to reflect. He remembered what had initially drawn him into the dream of community organizing, of bringing together all the congregations in town as part of a coalition. A certain phrase had stayed with him: "revolutionary love." Not just "revolutionary" and not just "love," but the two together. It was having faith that love could produce change. He hadn't been feeling or expressing much love at all lately. But he made up his mind that his resentment of the group in the larger city didn't serve justice. It didn't serve anything, actually. Joe decided: No matter what came next, he was going to uphold a spirit of revolutionary love.

> *Revolutionary love is a well-spring of care,*
> *an awakening to the inherent dignity*
> *and beauty of others and the earth, a quieting*
> *of the ego, a way of moving through the world*
> *in relationship, asking: 'What is your story?*
> *What is at stake? What is my part in your*
> *flourishing?' Loving others, even our opponents,*
> *in this way has the power to sustain political,*
> *social and moral transformation. This is*
> *how love changes the world.*

–VALARIE KAUR, FILMMAKER AND ACTIVIST

TRY THIS

Think of two or three values you intend to uphold, such as respect, kindness, or duty. If it's hard to think of some, try an Internet search of "examples of values." Now apply those values to your journey toward forgiveness. How does holding onto anger relate to those values? Does it strengthen and support them? Or weaken them? If you were to express these important values with regard to the person you're working to forgive, what would that look like? What would you do?

The Armor of the Lord's Prayer

Maria loved playing clarinet in the community band. Perfection wasn't required. Band members joked that with enough of them, they could cover the inevitable honks and squawks.

This lightheartedness was so different from her day job as a social worker, processing domestic violence cases for the state. That could wear a person down, day after day. Her wife said she needed something to help her lighten up. Thursday night band rehearsals were the perfect antidote.

Then Bert Caughman joined the percussion section. Maria had never met him before, but several years ago, she'd interviewed his ex-wife about his abusive behavior. The couple had gotten divorced, and he'd gone through court-mandated counseling sessions. But something about the presence of this man at rehearsals rankled her. What had been her refuge now seemed contaminated.

Even though he kept quiet and mostly to himself, he came to represent all the men who made her exhausting and heartbreaking work necessary. Professional ethics meant she couldn't tell anyone about him. She wasn't willing to quit the community band. Nor was she willing to spend rehearsals held hostage by her anger at him. She needed a way to handle it.

Maria turned to her long-held habit of prayer. Before getting out of the car and heading into rehearsal, she'd take a moment to say the Lord's Prayer. Instead of "Our Father," she'd once heard someone say, "Our Mother and Father," and that's what she did:

"Our Mother and Father, who art in heaven, hallowed be thy name. Thy kingdom come, thy will be done; on earth as it is in heaven. Give us this day our daily bread and forgive us our trespasses as we forgive those who trespass against us. Lead us not into temptation but deliver us from evil. For thine is the kingdom, and the power, and the glory, forever and ever. Amen."

Then she'd choose one phrase from the prayer to focus on for that evening. "Thy will be done," for example. Or "lead us not into temptation." She was not going to make Thursday evenings about Bert.

Now, when Bert shuffled his music or somehow caught her attention, she was better able to return to her chosen focal phrase from The Lord's Prayer. She wasn't letting him get in the way of her joy.

> 'Thy will be done' is what we are saying . . .
> We are asking God to be God. We are
> asking God to do not what we want, but
> what God wants . . . If it takes guts to face the
> omnipotence that is God's, it takes perhaps no
> less to face the impotence that is ours. We can
> do nothing without God. We can have nothing
> without God. Without God we are nothing.
>
> —FREDERICK BUECHNER

TRY THIS

Learn the Lord's Prayer by heart. Before a challenging situation, pray its words slowly. Then, choose an anchor phrase for the occasion, as Maria did. When anxiety or resentment arises, come back to the phrase. Find out what it means in that moment.

God of mercy and gentle strength,

God who loves me as I am,

I confess I have stumbled

In my desire to live in Your will.

Teach me to grow in wisdom and compassion,

So that I can learn to forgive

And greet the world in that patient spirit.

In Your Holy Name,

Amen.

Dealing with Unfinished Business

After years in Chicago, Ben and his wife, Mindy, were moving back to Iowa to take care of his parents and help run the family business, selling wholesale replacement parts for farm equipment. They were looking forward to getting away from the traffic. But Ben knew going home meant facing the congregation that had hurt him so deeply.

Growing up, he'd lived in constant fear of hell, as if God were around every corner waiting to pounce if he had a bad thought. Of course, especially as a teenager, he'd had doubts, flights of fancy, and plenty of sexual fantasies—the kinds of things the pastor always warned people about. Later on, in Chicago, a new church helped him understand God's mercy and forgiveness. But he'd stayed angry at his childhood church a long time.

Ben decided to pursue forgiveness in his usual methodical way. After a few weeks of reading and reflection, he invented a three-step process: Face It, Feel It, Free It.

In the first step, Face It, he recalled all the times someone had shamed him for deviating from the church's teachings. As he wrote it all out, he came to see that what he felt was less about one single event or another—it was the pervasive anxiety brought on by his experience in that church. He saw himself, as a child, shrinking away from God and trying to hide from God, rather than welcoming God, as he learned to do later.

Next up: Feel It. Even after years in the city, Ben was still his father's son—taciturn and reserved. Emotions in him didn't flow easily. But he was committed. So out on his evening walks, he'd try to open his heart to whatever feelings came up. The old familiar anger he'd tried to stuff away for so long would crop up. But there were also some surprises, like gratitude. Even if the pastor's words had taught him shame and fear, the congregants' neighborliness taught him precious lessons about community.

Then came the final step: Free It. Since he'd been a teenager, Ben had fantasized about returning to the congregation, flinging open the doors and denouncing the preacher. Or writing the perfect, Bible-anchored letter to prove, once and for all, just how wrong they were. Fairness had always been important to him. But that desire to punish them or prove them wrong was what he needed to release. By "free it," he meant something like "lose the attachment." It took many evening walks, whispering those words of release.

Several months later, when he and Mindy returned home, he was glad to see the members of the congregation. He would never have told them, but his ability to greet them so warmly had come from his ability, in the end, to decide to free it.

> *You can't forgive without loving. And I don't mean sentimentality. I don't mean mush. I mean having enough courage to stand up and say, 'I forgive. I'm finished with it.'*
>
> —MAYA ANGELOU

TRY THIS

Try to organize your process along these three steps: Face It, Feel It, Free It. Take the time to go through all three steps until you're free.

In Sight of the Bridge

When tragedy struck, people knew they could count on Linda to show up on the doorstep of any household experiencing fresh loss and know just what to do. Like so many others fluent in the ways of grief, it hadn't come easy for Linda. After her youngest son, Chris, had been killed in a drunk-driving accident, she'd gone through years of overwhelming grief. She still missed him, of course, but it was a gentler grief now. Her best friend, Kanesha, noted wryly that Linda had become the poster child for grief. It was true: She even gave talks about it. Although she had come to some peace about losing Chris, Linda still harbored a separate pain.

On that terrible night, an older boy named Robert had been at the wheel. He'd also died in the accident. A person couldn't be punished further, Linda thought. But, whenever she had to pass by the bridge where Robert and Chris died, or if she was watching a movie that had a teenage character with the same shock of black hair Robert had—if anything reminded her of him—the poison of bitterness would come seeping back. Although it didn't make sense, she almost wished he had lived so he could experience the consequence of what he'd done.

One night watching TV, she saw a story about how exposure therapy helps anxiety disorders. Instead of avoiding or escaping a triggering experience, exposure therapy was a means of engaging it. Not all at once—but little by little, like building up a tolerance. Linda got an idea.

The next day, on her lunch break, she drove to the part of town where the boys had died. She parked three blocks away from the bridge and ate her sandwich there. Yes, the old thoughts about Robert came up. But she saw she could handle it. The next day, she parked and ate her lunch one block closer. The third day, she parked her car within sight of the bridge. That was too much, she realized. She was unsettled the rest of the day and almost gave up. But a week later, she tried again. Yes, it was unpleasant. She felt that old anger about Robert's recklessness. But it was different. In a way, forgiveness was like grief—two steps forward, one step back. You couldn't predict how you'd feel, day to day, but you showed up. You kept at it. Within a month of that first lunch three blocks away, Linda and Kanesha went for a walk on the bridge. Linda hadn't been there in years. They stopped at the place where Chris and Robert had died and placed a few daisies.

"How are you feeling?" Kanesha said softly. Linda realized the old poison was weaker inside her than it ever had been. She was on her way to forgiveness.

> *The weak can never forgive. Forgiveness*
> *is an attribute of the strong.*
>
> —MAHATMA GANDHI

TRY THIS

Exposure therapy—incrementally engaging an emotional trigger—is one route toward forgiveness. Like other exercises in this book that intentionally allow challenging emotions to surface, finding a therapist or a clergyperson to facilitate reflection on the experiences can help. Technically speaking, since she's not working with a trained therapist, what Linda is doing in this story is not exposure therapy, but a homemade version of it. You can decide what version is right for you.

Living in Shalom

In late May 2020, when a white Minneapolis police officer murdered George Floyd, an African-American man, the whole nation woke up. For years prior to the murder, the extrajudicial killings of other Black people like Trayvon Martin and Philando Castile had roused many to take to the streets in grief and anger. They were calling out "Black Lives Matter!" in a country where it often seemed in doubt. But now, with protests growing, the statement that Black lives matter was no longer controversial in mainstream media channels. There were serious calls for new policies and new ways of ensuring community safety for every person. Yet for a country stained by the original sin of slavery, there was work to do to realize what in Hebrew is called *shalom*: the peace of wholeness. A central contention of this book is that this kind of peace can't be realized without forgiveness.

Even before securing reconciliation in the context of racism, what would forgiveness look like?

After the murder of George Floyd, there was a moment in Floyd's hometown of Houston. Under a shelter in the pouring rain, white and Black people gathered in obvious raw emotion. Without pre-planning—moved by the Spirit, as some would say—the white people knelt before the Black people. In the spirit of prayer, a man led a humble apology and asked forgiveness for their part in systemic racism.

Given the Internet age, when people can perform to create certain impressions, this moment might have come across as white people putting on a feel-good show. But, in the video of that moment, there is rawness in the voice of the white man as he prays for forgiveness. One of the Black men listening raises his eyes heavenward, seemingly overcome by emotion to hear, at long last, a white person apologize and seek forgiveness. That moment is a glimpse of *shalom*. Naming the harm done and expressing a desire to live in a different world isn't the completion of the work of forgiveness in community. It's not reconciliation. But God was in that moment, moving those hearts toward healing.

If my people who are called by my name humble themselves, pray, seek my face, and turn from their wicked ways, then I will hear from heaven, and will forgive their sin and heal their land.

2 CHRONICLES 7:14

CONSIDER THIS

1. If you are white, how have you sought cheap grace—the ease of good feeling without the acceptance and experience of suffering—regarding racism?

2. If you are white, what conditions would help you adopt a posture of humility with regard to racism? How would that humility and desire to seek forgiveness translate into sustained commitment, on your part, to seek racial healing in your community?

3. If you are BIPOC, given the eagerness for cheap grace by white people, forgiveness itself may be fraught with complication. What have you learned for yourself about what it takes to walk before God in faith, even amid the brutality of racism?

Summoning Your Elders

Jackie looked forward to attending the finance meetings at church. She even laughed about how crazy that was. What could sound more boring than a church finance meeting? But she loved her gritty, get-it-done church in the heart of downtown. The congregation was small but mighty, and people in the neighborhood knew they cared. If what they needed her to do was help with the finances, she was ready to go. She had a knack for numbers and had some ideas about how to improve a few processes. Unfortunately, her enthusiasm drained quickly. Stanley Hoover had chaired the finance committee for more than 20 years. He wasn't used to people showing up with new ideas and wasn't sure he liked it. So the fourth time Jackie butted in with an idea, Stanley's response wasn't very kind. She felt like she'd been stung by a bee—shocked and hurt.

Jackie left that meeting preoccupied. She was not accustomed to being treated like that. Plenty of civic organizations wanted her time, she told herself. She had other projects, like the quilt she was sewing for the guest room at home. She didn't need to spend her weeknights being barked at by Stanley Hoover. She was ready to quit, then remembered her promise to the pastor. When she'd joined the church four years ago, she said she wouldn't just be a worker bee. In whatever way God put her to work, she would commit to grow and learn from it. Well, what was there to learn in this case, she wondered, other than how to stomach another meeting with Stanley Hoover?!

Her pastor had always emphasized that although the church was poor in material resources, they were wealthy in wisdom. She decided to take this moment of hurt to do something other than quit or be angry. She would use it to enlarge her heart. Three older women came to mind, who were the epitome of wisdom: Eleanor, Sophie, and Virginia. They'd lived a long time and knew how to manage themselves well at church. Surely, they'd have some ideas about helping create a peaceful community and a peaceful heart within, even if what Stanley had done was inexcusable.

Sure enough, each of the older women had a different way to understand her situation. They each had stories to tell. Jackie took notes. It was nice to know that she wasn't alone in figuring out how to stay in a relationship within the congregation. Although she had officially joined the church a few years before, now she felt she really belonged. It was in the process of forgiveness that she made a deeper commitment from her heart to work through challenges. She planned to remain in a spirit of forgiveness.

> *To be a Christian means to forgive the inexcusable because God has forgiven the inexcusable in you.*
>
> −C. S. LEWIS

TRY THIS

Think of three people in your community you consider wise. Take your dilemma and your hurt to them, along with your intention to forgive, and talk to each person separately. Ask for guidance. Ask for their experience. What have they done in similar situations in life? Sift through what you hear. Make it your own. Apply it to your own situation.

The Grace of a Scapegoat

The Chicago Cubs hadn't won the World Series since 1908. It was now 2003 and things were looking good. It was the eighth inning in Game 6 of the National League Championship Series. The Cubs were up by three runs over the Florida Marlins, and by three games to two in a best of seven series. The National League pennant was in sight. As a foul ball hit by the Marlins' Luis Castillo drifted to the wall, the Cubbies left-fielder, Moisés Alou, had his glove up. Over his head, in the stands, everyone in the first few rows also reached up toward the ball. One of them, a man named Steve Bartman, reached too far over the edge and deflected the ball, which fell to the ground near Alou. Had Alou caught it, there would have been two outs—only four more to go to cinch the pennant. Instead, the Marlins caught fire and scored eight runs that inning. They beat the Cubs that night, eight to three. The next night, the Marlins won again and went on to win the World Series.

Right after Bartman obstructed Alou's catch, other Cubs fans in the stands began to scream and throw trash at him. It got so bad that security personnel had to escort Bartman from the stadium for his own safety.

The leak of his name and personal information online began years of harassment from Cubs fans who blamed him for their team's loss. Bartman publicly apologized and said he wanted to move beyond the incident, back to his quiet life in financial services. Cubs players also supported Bartman, taking responsibility for how things had turned out that season. But many fans weren't convinced. Bartman had become a scapegoat. The notoriety and harassment continued for years.

In 2016, at long last, the Cubs finally won the World Series. As a gesture of atonement of how he'd been treated, they ordered a World Series ring for Bartman. In response, Bartman made a rare public statement. He said, "Although I do not consider myself worthy of such an honor, I am deeply moved and sincerely grateful to receive an official Chicago Cubs 2016 World Series Championship ring." He went on, "I am happy to be reunited with the Cubs family and positively moving forward with my life."

Steve Bartman could have expressed bitterness for years of harassment. But, in response to such efforts at reconciliation, he effectively brought the unfortunate chapter in sports history to an end.

Now if anyone has caused pain, he has caused it not to me, but in some measure—not to put it too severely—to all of you. For such a one, this punishment by the majority is enough, so you should rather turn to forgive and comfort him, or he may be overwhelmed by excessive sorrow. So I beg you to reaffirm your love for him . . . Anyone whom you forgive, I also forgive.

2 CORINTHIANS 2:5-8, 10

TRY THIS

Forgiveness (within oneself) is not the same as reconciliation (between parties). But if someone has been hoping for your forgiveness, and you have realized forgiveness within yourself, how could you express it to that person, to let them know? Steve Bartman made a rare public statement. Think of how you would communicate forgiveness in a way that's true to you.

The steady injection of compassion into community and community relationships raises the community immune system. Even when problems persist, when the suffering of the other person can be named and honored, it's possible for us all to find our way peacefully. Compassion, in this sense, is not only an interpersonal quality. It's a cultural value in your congregation, your club, your neighborhood.

Two years ago, someone down the street hung a Confederate flag in his window. A neighbor, who is an African-American woman, asked me to go talk with the man about taking it down. She mentioned the negative effect it had on her children. I was moved, thinking about the effect of normalizing that terrible symbol on my own children, too.

A few days later, I walked over to the man's house, with some fresh-baked banana bread, wrapped in foil. He was in his carport, working on a project. I've lived in the South most of my life and have no patience for excusing the Confederate flag. But I did have compassion for this man in the carport. As we talked, his conscience was stirred. The next day the flag came down. I'm convinced that, because our exchange was conducted in a spirit of compassion, he was able to choose to do the right thing. For all I know, the banana bread helped. Different outcomes can come from interactions like that. But I'll stick with compassion, engaging my community as a follower of Jesus, as one who knows God.

WHEN YOU ARE COMPASSIONATE
WITH YOURSELF, YOU TRUST IN YOUR
SOUL . . . WHICH YOU LET GUIDE
YOUR LIFE. YOUR SOUL KNOWS
THE GEOGRAPHY OF YOUR DESTINY
BETTER THAN YOU DO.

–JOHN O'DONOHUE, IRISH POET AND PRIEST

CHAPTER 6

SELF

Kristin Neff is an associate professor of human development at the University of Texas and a pioneer in the field of self-compassion. It was Dr. Neff who developed the 26-point "self-compassion scale," which measures how compassionate or judgmental people are to themselves. You might think it's easy to be compassionate toward yourself. But Dr. Neff has found otherwise. In a *New York Times* article, she said, "I found in my research that the biggest reason people aren't more self-compassionate is that they are afraid they'll become self-indulgent." She went on, "They believe self-criticism is what keeps them in line. Most people have gotten it wrong because our culture says being hard on yourself is the way to be."

When you've hurt someone else, the mature thing to do is to take responsibility. But that responsibility can curdle, becoming a deep-set sense of guilt, and even shame. Although the impulse begins in empathy, carrying the burden of our impact on others for too long without moving toward healing can be counterproductive to others and to ourselves. Throughout this book, we have explored ways of moving toward healing in relationships with others. But perhaps the most challenging relationship in which to practice forgiveness is with yourself. As Dr. Neff suggests, you can imagine that to withhold forgiveness from yourself is somehow virtuous. It's as if you believe you wouldn't do the right thing without some penalty to yourself.

That's psychologically wrongheaded. It's also theologically unsound. There is a view that says that God is angry and punishing—and, if we are to be faithful, we should be likewise harsh in our conduct and self-understanding. It's easy to see how that view of fundamental unworthiness would lead you to believe you need to drive yourself to "earn" your worthiness—through overexertion and scoring holy "brownie points" or through suffering in some way that seems noble, like withholding forgiveness from yourself. There's just one problem. That self-punishing worldview has nothing to do with the loving and merciful God as attested to in scripture and experienced by the faithful since time immemorial. For instance, the 14th-century mystic, Julian of Norwich, experienced a very loving God. While living through times of plague and tragedy, he said this about God's unconditional love for us: "If there is anywhere on earth a lover of God who is always kept safe, I know nothing of it, for it was not shown to me. But this was shown: that in falling and rising again we are always kept in that same precious love."

Trusting in that same precious love that God has for you, you are not only invited to consider self-forgiveness, you are compelled to forgive yourself, that you may remove any obstacle to fully loving God.

ACTS: A Clear Way to Pray

Recently, Jeanne dreaded hearing from her eldest daughter. Beth was almost 30 years old, well-launched in her career, and dating a nice young woman in a relationship that seemed serious. But Beth's new therapist had been encouraging her to confront Jeanne about certain aspects of growing up. Beth's main complaint was that Jeanne hadn't been emotionally available for her during some difficult teenage years. Beth talked about it with raw emotion, and Jeanne did her best to listen, but she couldn't help feeling defensive. She'd been a single mom, and some days it had felt like an accomplishment just to have everyone fed and clothed. Beth's calls had been coming in waves for three months, often when Beth was driving home from her therapist's office. She was always accusatory, always in tears.

Jeanne started doubting her own parenting. Had she damaged her girls? She began to feel a tightness in her chest, like her heart had turned into a fist. Sometimes, on these calls, she got panicky, knowing there was nothing she could do to change the past.

At the Moose Lodge, Jeanne was known for cracking jokes. But people started to notice her recent glum expression. Her friend Casey got the truth out of her, and told her to cut herself some slack. But it wasn't that easy. Two weeks later, Casey said, "Okay, my friend. I know people don't like it when people get in their business about faith. And I know you don't go to church. But can I teach you something?"

They'd been friends for a long time, so Jeanne said cautiously, "Sure."

On the back of a napkin, Casey wrote the letters A C T S. "Acts," she said. "It's a way to talk to God." She had learned it at church as a way to pray when your brain was scrambled.

The "A" was for "adoration"—when you call God by name, in a way that felt true.

The "C" was for "confession"—when you share whatever you want about yourself or what you'd done.

The "T" was for "thanksgiving"—for all the mercy and grace you have already enjoyed.

The "S" was for "supplication"—when you humbly ask for God's intervention in the face of some challenge.

"For example," said Casey, "when your daughter is guilt-tripping you every week about this or that."

Jeanne laughed at Casey's frank talk. She folded the napkin and put it in her purse. In the weeks after, she began to pray, following the ACTS template. She asked God to ease Beth's pain about her childhood. She asked God to help her forgive herself for not being the mother she wished she would have been. It was not a fast-acting pill or a magic bullet. But this new practice, following this manner of prayer, brought Jeanne self-forgiveness regarding her parenting. She gained a broader sense of grace. The peace people feel when they have invited God's mercy into their lives now radiated from her.

Do not worry about anything, but in everything by prayer and supplication with thanksgiving let your requests be made known to God. And the peace of God, which surpasses all understanding, will guard your hearts and your minds in Christ Jesus.

PHILIPPIANS 4:6-7

TRY THIS

ACTS is a simple mnemonic device that can help people pray. Follow Casey's outline, and see what it's like when you pray in that way, making sure you stay kind to yourself.

Befriending Yourself

Coach Jackson loved Halloween almost as much as he loved basketball. In early September, he'd begin planning and collecting supplies for the holiday. His house was known throughout the city for the ornate decorations—the rubber masks hung in trees, the strobe light he'd set up in the woods, the sound of shrieking ghosts that came from his porch. His wife teased him a little, asking when he was going to finally outgrow it. But he would just laugh and tell her about the new plans he had for next year. Then, the accident happened.

Tim Arnold was 12 years old. No one knew why, but he climbed a ladder Coach Jackson had left up against a tree in his backyard for hanging decorations, and had fallen off. He'd spent a couple of nights in the hospital, but the doctors said he'd be okay. Coach Jackson, on the other hand, could not let it go. He was a precise man, accustomed to planning ahead and getting the details right. He preached as much to his team every year on the basketball court. But here he had failed a basic guideline of safety: to ensure that a place was safe before leaving it. And now a child was hurt because of his failure.

Coach knew he could be uncompromising and even harsh with his players and with himself. That's what happened now. Even after he'd talked with Tim Arnold's family, and had been assured that Tim would be fine in the long run, he couldn't shake his anger with himself. "Careless," he muttered, as he worked in the yard. "Stupid," he hissed, driving to get groceries.

Luckily, one of Coach Jackson's habits was research. One night, after a few weeks had gone by, he stayed up late searching the Internet. He found a study published by researchers at the University of Arizona; it found that people who spoke kindly to themselves in the months after divorce score higher on mental health tests than those who speak harshly to themselves. Coach Jackson wasn't going through a divorce, but he did want to stop punishing himself for having left out the ladder. This research agreed with his experience coaching teenagers. Even though he could be critical, he'd seen how praise and encouragement of the desired behavior—extra effort, sportsmanship, and so forth—had a greater effect than criticism.

Coach began to reconsider the episode with the ladder. Although he wished he hadn't left it out, he realized he was human and that it was a simple mistake. He reflected on the overall positive nature of his Halloween decor. And how Tim Arnold's family (and Tim himself) had been so forgiving. In the days afterward, when he caught himself playing the loop of negative self-talk, he began to override it with caring affirmation. As he did, he experienced greater ease. By Christmas, his feelings had followed his kind words, and he was eager to start setting up his Christmas decorations . . . which were only second in extravagance to those for Halloween.

> *Self-rejection is the greatest enemy of the spiritual life because it contradicts the sacred voice that calls us the "Beloved."*
>
> —HENRI NOUWEN

TRY THIS

Notice how you talk to yourself. Is it kind? Unkind? See if you can intentionally change the script of your self-talk to one saturated with self-compassion. If you find yourself using negative self-talk, stop and rewind. Replay the thought with positive feedback. Instead of "You're so stupid for erasing that file," think "Erasing that file was unfortunate, but it doesn't make me stupid. There are other good things I've done today, like replying to all those emails."

Self-Compassion Through Service

Jane fired a young man named Wesley Berkman three months ago, but the decision still weighed on her. She found herself cyberstalking him, to see if he had found a new job. He hadn't. Jane had been in management almost 15 years. She had fired dozens and dozens of people. She liked to be direct. She considered it transparent and fair. But when she had talked with Wesley on that day three months ago, he had been visibly upset. He blurted out, "But what will I do?" There was something so open and plaintive in the question. She'd felt terrible about it.

Intellectually, she knew she was clear in her expectations and followed through without bias. Her company depended on her for results from high standards. Sometimes, it meant firing people. But never had she been so aware of the impact on someone else's life. Online, she saw pictures of Wesley's two little kids and friendly looking wife. How were they eating? Did the wife have a job?

Jane wondered if she needed to get out of management. She remembered her old mentor, Peggy Ramsey, who'd always invite young Jane into her office to debrief after yet one more mistake. In those days it seemed like Jane was always making mistakes. How had Peggy gotten such results—hitting her target each quarter—with such an easy-going style? Maybe Jane just wasn't cut out for all of this. Or maybe she just didn't want to live with the burden of making decisions that can have such an effect on other people. She didn't want to be the Wicked Witch of the West anymore.

Jane's brother knew she was going through some career discernment, so he suggested she try volunteering. Jane decided to give it a shot. A nearby elementary school needed tutors for third-graders, two hours a week. Jane went on Mondays after work and was paired with a boy named Oliver. She saw how he struggled with math in particular. Her heart went out to him. She realized that when she got impatient, he would shut down. So she practiced being patient with him, and sharing her compassion in the form of little encouraging remarks.

It certainly had not been her intent, but over these Monday visits, as her compassion for Oliver grew, her compassion for herself grew, as well. In time, she developed some management innovations, including programs to help displaced employees find their next job. But she also found herself "riding easier in the saddle," as she put it. Her job would still ask her to fire people from time to time. But it was part of the job, and she made the best of it. Her compassion for others had taught her compassion for herself.

You shall love your neighbor as yourself.

MARK 12:31B

TRY THIS

If you have been stuck in self-blame for some time, see what difference it makes to serve others, to cultivate compassion for them. Developing that capacity in your heart for others can help forgiveness for yourself come more easily.

Self-Soothing Through Touch

Marcie moved like a whirlwind through the living room, picking up pens, candy wrappers, and Legos while her kids hid themselves in their bedrooms. She didn't blame them. When she got amped-up like this and couldn't sit still, she didn't want to be around herself either. Some days were worse than others. She never knew when it would hit: the memory of the two kids standing by the road with their goat.

A few years prior, Marcie had been deployed to Iraq. Her battalion was locking down a village outside Ramadi, and she was going from house to house with a team of other soldiers to secure the village, with an eye out for insurgents. That's when she'd seen the two kids with their goat. They couldn't have been more than seven years old. They stood wide-eyed, staring at the American soldiers. She didn't see exactly what happened—a young man in one house made a sudden move, the report said—but there was a sudden exchange of gunfire. The whole thing lasted less than a minute. After, looking around, not only did she see a young man dead in the street, she saw the bodies of those children. Their goat was running around in a panic, his rope loose.

Since then, there were a lot of days when Marcie felt like that goat, running around in a panic. If she could stay busy, the images didn't come up as much. It was hard to keep the terrible sense of guilt at bay, and the cascade of "if onlys": if only she had thrown her body over the kids to protect them, if only she had gotten her buddy to go down another street. If only, if only. She knew she couldn't change the past. But she couldn't stop paying for it.

She went to see a therapist who focused on what happens in the body after an experience like the one she had. She told Marcie that it wasn't only mental or emotional, it was physiological. What Marcie thought of as being amped-up was really her sympathetic nervous system—her fight-or-flight response—revving into gear. Even though a lot of counseling had helped Marcie make some sense of the day, the experience was still stuck in her body.

The therapist recommended a couple of things to try the next time the memory flared up. The first was to put her hand on her heart and to take a few deep breaths. Or she could rest her hand gently on another part of her body, such as her face or arm. Marcie knew that laying a hand on her children's backs would help them when they were having trouble going to sleep. This was the same thing, really, "gentling" herself down. Over time, she noticed that she was able to move to a different level of peace with what happened. Yes, she would spend her life thinking of how to honor the lives of those children. But no longer would she be haunted by them, or all she hadn't done. Forgiving herself was the only way to move on.

> *If you can't forgive yourself, you'll always*
> *be an exile in your own life.*
>
> —CURTIS SITTENFELD

TRY THIS

When an unforgiving feeling flares up, try to self-soothe with some gentle touch, as described in Marcie's story. Imagine how you would express care for someone else with a calming touch. Care for yourself in exactly the same way.

Receiving God's Gifts

As his college reunion drew near, Bart felt worse and worse. His wife, Kay, was baffled. "These are the guys you've been talking about now for years. And you don't want to go? I don't get it."

Reunions are a time of reckoning and, now at age 41, Bart felt lousy about what he'd done with his life. Worse, he knew his old roommate Peter would be there. Peter was the one who'd remind him about how badly he'd messed up his life. Peter had been an entrepreneur even in college, selling vintage postcards out of their dorm room. On graduation, he asked if Bart wanted to invest in the company he was starting up, selling collectibles online. Bart declined. At the time, $1,000 seemed like a lot of money. Two years later, as Peter's business continued to grow, he reached out again. Did Bart want to come work with him? Again, Bart declined. To exchange a steady paycheck for the uncertain prospect of working for a business still finding its feet seemed too big a risk.

As the years passed, Bart's career stagnated—not only his finances, but also his own sense of meaning and growth. Meanwhile, Peter seemed to flourish in every way possible. Bart had made what he thought was a safe bet, and it had cost him dearly. He wished he could provide Kay with a beach vacation or a car that didn't sound like a garbage can rolling down the street.

Finally, he confessed to Kay what had been eating at him. She laughed a bit. She said, "Well, I like our little life. I like our old blender that doesn't work unless you hold down the lid while it runs. I like our little house. I don't need beach vacations. Here's what I think. I think God has blessed us richly, if we only look around. But that's how I see it. Have you prayed about this?"

Of course, Bart hadn't. Whenever he got anxious and insecure, he seemed to forget to pray. So he took this burden to prayer. God, he figured out, was less concerned with his bank account than with the state of his heart. Sure, he wasn't rich. And maybe he had passed up great opportunities with Peter twice. But God wasn't punishing him. God was blessing him. He just hadn't seen it.

A month later at the reunion, Peter picked up the check at the restaurant for everyone. But what impressed people the most was the peace and joy that seemed to radiate from Bart, who had a depth and contentment others envied.

I think that if God forgives us we must forgive ourselves. Otherwise, it is almost like setting up ourselves as a higher tribunal than Him.

—C. S. LEWIS

TRY THIS

Sometimes, we can't forgive ourselves for decisions we've made, given how they affected the way our lives turned out. The religious scholar, Joseph Campbell, once said, "We must be willing to get rid of the life we've planned, so as to have the life that is waiting for us." In that spirit, look at your current life in a new light. See it not as a curse or an accident, but exactly as it should be. Can you see the blessings you've received—not *despite* things being as they are but *because* of them? What do you notice that you hadn't before? How does what you haven't forgiven yourself for now appear in that light?

Praise and Thanksgiving for the God Who Has Known
and Loved Us from the Start
For it was you who formed my inward parts;
you knit me together in my mother's womb.
I praise you, for I am fearfully and wonderfully made.
Wonderful are your works;
that I know very well.
My frame was not hidden from you,
when I was being made in secret,
intricately woven in the depths of the earth.
Your eyes beheld my unformed substance.
In your book were written
all the days that were formed for me,
when none of them as yet existed.
Psalm 139:13-16

One Hundred Examples of Positive Proof

Jack was forgetful by nature, his head always in the clouds. But when his wife, Tonya, discovered he'd forgotten to buy their plane tickets to Los Angeles one week before they were supposed to depart, she lost it. "How could you?" she cried. "We've been saving all year. The hotels are booked. The car is rented!" Jack didn't know what to say. It had just slipped his mind.

Tonya said she was going to go on a walk. When she came back, she had figured out a solution and got to work. A friend who worked in the travel industry managed to find them a relatively affordable flight. Their trip was back on.

Tonya and Jack made peace, but Jack laid awake that night, feeling miserable. This wasn't the only important thing he'd forgotten. He regularly forgot to bring home items from the grocery store. He forgot birthdays. It had been like this his whole life—details and facts seemed to float away from him.

The next day, he was still in a funk. He tried to hide it from Tonya. It was his problem, after all. He didn't need to burden her with it. But what to do? He had read all the books about getting organized. He had tried to be different. But he seemed doomed to wander the world this way.

Tonya found him brooding out on the porch. "Beating yourself up again?" she asked quietly.

He nodded. They'd had this conversation before.

"Well," she said playfully. "I'm going to Los Angeles in a few days to have fun, and I don't want my travel companion to be in a funk. So what are we going to do?"

Jack shrugged. He didn't want to be dramatic, but it was hard to shake what a screw-up he was. Tonya disappeared into the house, then returned with a pad of paper and a pen. "Here," she said. "I want you to do something." He looked up. She said, "Write down 100 things you have done in the last week that have made a positive difference in the world."

He sighed. This was not where his mind was. But he'd give it a try.

He began with number one: rolled the neighbor's garbage can to the street on trash day. Number two: sent a funny card to his niece. By about number 34, he began to slow down. But he kept at it. When he reached 100, he read the whole list. This was not the behavior of an unsalvageable screw-up! Yes, he was forgetful, and his lapses sometimes had a negative impact on others. But, as the list showed, he also did some good. He wasn't beyond redemption. It was good to get perspective. It allowed him to see himself as neither a hero nor a lost cause, but a human who was wired in a particular way, doing the best he could.

*But do not ignore this one fact, beloved,
that with the Lord one day is like a thousand years,
and a thousand years are like one day. The Lord is not
slow about his promise, as some think of slowness,
but is patient with you, not wanting any to perish,
but all to come to repentance.*

2 PETER 3:8-9

TRY THIS

Like Jack, make a list of 100 things you've done that have had a positive impact. See how it shifts your perspective. Give yourself at least three compliments about the positive effect you are having. Congratulate yourself on reading this book and putting it into action!

Singing to Heal

Amanda knew her brother Evan thought about suicide. He had a dark sense of humor about it, calling it his Plan B. He'd talked about doing it for so long, without acting on it, that it was a surprise one evening when the phone call finally came. Her sweet, funny brother was dead, leaving his wife and two children. Something wild broke loose inside Amanda. She wanted to scream loud enough that the whole world would stand still. Even after the funeral, when she had read all the books about grief and knew that guilt was part of what she was feeling, she couldn't escape a sense of responsibility. She should have found a way to stop him. It was like she'd been watching a slow-moving train wreck that took 34 years to complete. In all that time, surely, she could have done something. Her old excuses hardly seemed like enough. It was, quite literally, a matter of life and death. And she hadn't saved him. She hadn't been vigilant enough. She let him slip away.

Around then, her friend Hannah invited her to choir practice. It was in an old church downtown, and the choir had shrunk to nine people, most of whom were older than 80. Amanda loved it. It felt great being around these sweet older people, under the high ornate stone ceiling, with the view of vast stained-glass windows. And, of course, there was the singing.

She especially loved one piece called "*Te Deum laudamus*" or "We praise you, God." Although it had been arranged by a modern composer, she loved that it went back centuries, as if she was now joining voices not only with the other choir members, but with generations of people who had once gathered to praise God. She'd never been able to pray in a way that made sense to her, and she found reading the Bible confusing. But now, in this moment of grief and self-flagellation, singing ancient songs of praise delivered her into the presence of grace. As she sang "*Te Deum laudamus*" she felt an intimacy with a

God who knew about weeping and suffering and tears, and could hold them all—could hold the ocean of tears within her—without flinching from either the pain or the hope of some redemption.

Years later, when people learned that her brother had ended his life and wanted to know what had helped her in those times, she would tell them about the choir. She would relay how singing helped her open back up from guilt and self-recrimination to find a place of acceptance and peace.

I will sing to the Lord as long as I live;
I will sing praise to my God while I have being.

PSALM 104:33

TRY THIS

Singing songs of faith can help cultivate a forgiving heart. Maybe, like Amanda, ancient songs invite you to sing. Perhaps traditional ones like "Amazing Grace" speak to you. Maybe you prefer modern praise songs, like "Grateful" by Hezekiah Walker. (You can find any of these on YouTube.) You can sing in church, join a choir, or belt it out in your kitchen if you can't carry a tune. The idea is not professional polish, but to let yourself be an honest channel of the Spirit.

Loving All That You Are

For a year, Ben carried on an on-again, off-again affair with Darcey, another social worker at his agency. Each time he was with her, he swore it would be the last time. He was an adult man; he knew he was responsible for it. So he confessed to Emily, his wife of five years. He had fantasized that she would forgive him, and they'd go to counseling. He envisioned the "long road to healing" that supermarket magazines talked about. But there was none of that. Emily heard the news, walked out of their apartment, and then returned to announce that their marriage was over. Her voice trembled as she said it, but her decision was firm.

Now his friends and family all knew about the affair; so did Emily's family, who had admired him so much before. His whole life, he'd always been "the good guy"—he was a social worker, for crying out loud! And here he was, walking the world as the villain in his story, the reason for the breakup of a marriage that had made everyone envious. Emily told him how much the broken trust had hurt her, and how she didn't know if she could ever trust another person again. He wasn't sure how his movie would end. He'd apologized to Emily. He'd apologized to Darcey. He'd apologized to his friends and family and to Emily's family for the hurt he'd caused. But he didn't know how to come to peace in himself. The months of deception, of withholding the truth from his wife, ate away at him. It was not the behavior of the kind of man he'd thought he was. But he had to face up to the fact that he had no one to blame but himself.

How ever life would go on, he realized, it couldn't be with him as "the good guy" anymore. Not only had he been publicly proven a liar and a cheat, he was realizing that maintaining a façade didn't help anyone, including him. His eagerness for others' approval made him manipulative. He wanted to be more honest now. He needed to be accepted and loved—by others and by himself—as the flawed person he was.

He began to write in his journal every morning, being more honest about his life patterns than he ever had been. When he was done writing a page or two, he'd lay his hand on what he'd written and say, out loud, "I love this part of Ben, too." It took time and didn't erase the impact of what he'd done. But this was how his path toward self-forgiveness began.

A fish cannot drown in water,
A bird does not fall in air.
In the fire of creation,
God doesn't vanish:
The fire brightens.
Each creature God made
must live in its own true nature;
How could I resist my nature,
That lives for oneness with God?

—MECHTHILD OF MAGDEBURG, MEDIEVAL MYSTIC AND WRITER

TRY THIS

Take up a journaling practice, even if just for one day. Write as honestly as you can. Commit to telling the truth about all that you've done, all that you are, and how you have hurt other people. When you're done writing, lay your hand over what you've written and commit to loving the person responsible for all that. You are worthy of forgiveness; you are worthy of love.

Committing to Counterbalance the Harm

In middle school, Damon had been a class clown. He was athletically challenged and a half step out of fashion, but when he got people laughing, there was nothing like it. Unfortunately, his jokes were almost always at another kid's expense. One friend named Charles was overweight and spoke in a high-pitched voice. Damon was able to develop an impression of Charles that the popular kids loved. It was more than 30 years ago, but Damon still shamefully remembers the look on Charles's face when he'd come around the corner to see Damon doing his impression while all the other kids laughed. That had finally ended Damon's middle school comedy career. Charles never spoke to him again, and they lost touch after high school.

Damon went on to lead a normal life. He was happily married and a good dad to his kids. But his cruelty as a child gnawed at his conscience. He couldn't lay it to rest. When one of his kids mentioned some bullying at school, Damon felt a surge of anger. He said, "Don't they know how awful that is?" He knew his anger was not about his kid's schoolmates; it was from his own guilt from so long ago.

One day, Damon had an idea. He found an organization that coordinated antibullying programming in his area. After a conversation with the executive director, he decided to make a monthly donation to support their work. He couldn't change the past or erase whatever effect he'd had on Charles's life. He knew he couldn't purchase redemption—grace is freely given from God. But this was a relevant way to contribute toward a force of good. A way of working toward making amends. He never told anyone, other than his wife. And he did a lot of ongoing reflection about what it was that had made him be so cruel as a child for the reward of fleeting popularity.

As a child he may have taken delight in mockery and domination. Contributing to this antibullying agency was a monthly reminder of the humility he sought now to maintain.

Three times I appealed to the Lord about this, that [a thorn in my flesh] would leave me, but he said to me, "My grace is sufficient for you, for power is made perfect in weakness." So, I will boast all the more gladly of my weaknesses, so that the power of Christ may dwell in me. Therefore, I am content with weaknesses, insults, hardships, persecutions, and calamities for the sake of Christ; for whenever I am weak, then I am strong.

2 CORINTHIANS 12:8-10

TRY THIS

While maintaining a wariness of your desire to erase or compensate for the injury you have caused—for you can't erase the past, only shift your relationship to it—consider how you might make some effort to counterbalance the harm you have done. This is not reconciliation; you are not making peace in relationship with the other person. But it may bring you some inward peace. Choose a commitment that signals how you desire to live as you move forward in your life.

The Past Is the Past

Gayle had a rough childhood. When Ken came along at age 19, with big plans, she had hopped aboard, eager to join him on his journey. Unfortunately, Ken was never meant to go far. He didn't even leave town. They settled down, had three kids, and became further and further entrenched in the struggles of daily life. It was only in her mid-40s, as the kids began to fly the coop, that Gayle thought to ask what she wanted from life. She'd always done what was good for her family, or what was good for Ken. What was good for her? She didn't know how to answer.

Little by little, she discovered she had a knack for photography and graphic design. She earned a certificate from the community college and was hired by local businesses for various projects. She liked the creativity and the respect people showed her. She liked pulling in a paycheck. She wasn't sure where things were going with Ken at this stage of their life and marriage, now that the intensity of parenting was over. Since taking her graphic design business more seriously, she couldn't escape the feeling of fierce regret that bubbled up like lava inside. Like she'd missed something big. Her 20s and 30s and half of her 40s were already over! What a fool she had been. Could she have moved to New York? Could she have had a completely different life? Now she would never know.

One night, she and Ken were cutting up vegetables for a salad. The TV was on. She had mentioned, here and there, some of what she was feeling. But now she let it all out. The bitter regret. The judgment of how much she had sacrificed. Ken kept chopping vegetables. He was a quiet man. When her torrent of words died down a little, she said, "Does anything I'm saying to you make any sense?"

He thought a minute, then said, "Well, I guess I just figure the past is the past and the future is the future."

Such simple words, but, for Gayle, it changed everything. She had been ruminating so much on her wasted 20s and 30s—angry about her decisions, angry at the person living through those years without direction. All that rumination began to threaten the rest of her 40s, her 50s, and beyond. Why should she let it? From that point on, when she would start to get hung up on missed chances, she would whisper to herself, "The past is the past." Somehow that would shift things inside for her, and she would reorient herself to the life she intended to lead in the years ahead.

> *For everything there is a season, and*
> *a time for every matter under heaven.*
> ECCLESIASTES 3:1

TRY THIS

On a piece of paper, draw a line down the center. On top of the left column, write, "Can't be changed." Over the right column, write, "Still possible." See if you can fill up both columns. Flip the page over and continue your lists, if necessary. Often, forgiveness gets stuck with confusion about what can be changed and what can't. How do your lists change your perspective?

You already know that maintaining a self-punishing stance doesn't feel good emotionally. But chronic stress from avoiding self-forgiveness can also affect your physical, mental, and spiritual health. Cultivating compassion and forgiveness not only releases us from that damaging cycle of pain, but allows us to be of service to others. In fact, for having been through the "valley of the shadow of death" and emerged, healed, our service to others and our life of faith will embody the humility of what spiritual teacher Henri Nouwen called "the wounded healer." He wrote, "Our service will not be perceived as authentic unless it comes from a heart wounded by the suffering about which we speak." I've seen that time and again: The ways in which we have suffered become the ways in which we can serve. I know a man who grew up steeped in the poison of unapologetic white supremacist culture. As he escaped from that worldview, he found his life's work: to help other white people recover from the delusion of white supremacy. Another woman I know suffered from postpartum depression; now, she's known as a resource in the community for other moms. Their service is perceived as authentic, Henri Nouwen would say, because it comes from a heart wounded by the suffering about which they speak. Through the hard, brave work of healing in self-forgiveness, you can become a source of wisdom and compassion to others, as well.

Maintaining Your Forgiving Mind

In this book, you've engaged 60 different ways of cultivating a forgiving heart. Forgiveness, you've seen, is a creative process and practice. It's not a one-and-done, quick-fix endeavor. Through your efforts and your commitment to develop forgiveness, a day will arrive when you notice you're no longer burdened in the way you once were. Yes, your past experiences will affect your future, but you will not be bound by them any longer. Although the early practice of forgiveness can build your emotional and spiritual "immune system," realistically there will be relapses here and there. An encounter with the one who hurt you, or an environment similar to the one in which you were hurt, could trigger the rise of old feelings. Your capacity to respond will be linked not only to your general wellness—your sleep, anxiety levels, and overall outlook—but also to the extent to which you've maintained an active practice of forgiveness.

What could a "maintenance" program of forgiveness look like? Just like physical exercise, the most effective strategy is to practice the exercises that work best for you. Don't focus on the ones you or others feel you "should" pursue. Pick the ones you've tried or the ones you are most likely to stick with. Different exercises will appeal to different people. Of all the exercises in this book, there may be, say, 20 that have especially resonated for you. From those 20, you might choose three, at first, to work on intentionally.

When the inevitable upsets arise, rejoice! It means you're still alive and able to feel. Those upsets are the opportunities to practice your forgiving heart.

When we're in pain, we're motivated to change. When you first picked up this book, before you did any exercises, you might have been eager to try *anything* that would relieve you of suffering. An ongoing maintenance program, however, can be a challenge.

One successful strategy for incorporating a new habit is through "scaffolding." Scaffolding is the strategy of tacking on one new habit to your current, established habits. For instance, you have any number of daily habits: coffee in the morning, going for a walk at lunch, brushing your teeth before bed. If you brush your teeth before bed at night, you might decide that immediately after finishing, you'll take a moment to pray using the ACTS exercise (pages 121–122). Or, when enjoying your first cup of morning coffee, you might add the habit of gratitude journaling, as described on page 137. Your personalized exercises, integrated into your established habits, will form an ongoing forgiveness practice that deepens your faith and strengthens your heart for the years ahead.

As time goes on, this book will continue to be a resource, offering new ways to meet new challenges that arise. Come back and reread chapters or reconsider practices to meet any challenge with a forgiving heart.

Resources

Books

All About Love: New Visions (Love Song to the Nation) by bell hooks
This book by feminist bell hooks takes a new look at love in a polarized time.

Immunity to Change: How to Overcome It and Unlock the Potential in Yourself and Your Organization by Robert Kegan and Lisa Laskow Lahey
This book can help you work through your resistance to forgive.

Self-Compassion: The Proven Power of Being Kind to Yourself by Kristin Neff
A book by a leading researcher of self-compassion.

To Bless the Space Between Us by John O'Donohue
A book of lyrical blessings that can be read as prayers or used to offer blessings to others in your forgiveness journey.

Organizations

The Bowen Center for the Study of the Family. TheBowenCenter.org
This center in Washington, DC, offers training and programs on family systems, and promotes greater individual clarity and maturity in relations with others.

The Center for Action and Contemplation. CAC.org

Founded by Richard Rohr, the CAC offers spiritual development training for engaged, Jesus-following lives.

The Charter for Compassion. CharterForCompassion.org

Religious scholar Karen Armstrong and others have promoted this organization as a common-ground, compassion-based agenda for communities.

The Forgiveness Toolbox. TheForgivenessToolbox.com

This website offers resources and exercises that help identify skills that can be applied to forgiveness.

Lombard Mennonite Peace Center. LMPeaceCenter.org

This center offers skills and practices of peace in the community setting.

The Midwest Institute for Forgiveness Training. ForgivenessTraining.com

Their programs and interventions are for those who want a more facilitated experience toward forgiveness.

Revolutionary Love Conference. RevolutionaryLoveConference.com

An annual revival for progressive Christians at the Middle Collegiate Church in New York City. The worship and programs often include a dimension of forgiveness.

References

Bible in One Year. "Experience the relief of forgiveness." Accessed
August 8, 2020. BibleInOneYear.org/bioy/commentary/2473.

Billheimer, John. *Baseball and the Blame Game: Scapegoating in the
Major Leagues.* McFarland & Company, 2007.

Blake, William. *The Complete Poetry and Prose of William Blake.*
Berkeley, CA: University of California Press, 2008.

Boggs, Grace Lee. *The Next American Revolution: Sustainable
Activism for the Twenty-First Century.* 1st ed. Berkeley, CA:
University of California Press, 2012.

Bradford Cannon, Walter B. *The Wisdom of the Body.* New York, NY:
W. W. Norton and Company, Inc., 1963.

Brainy Quote. Accessed August 28, 2020. BrainyQuote.com/quotes
/ben_okri_393732.

Brainy Quote. Accessed August 27, 2020. BrainyQuote.com/quotes
/lewis_b_smedes_135524.

Brainy Quote. Accessed August 31, 2020. BrainyQuote.com/quotes
/t_d_jakes_488837.

Buechner, Frederick. *Whistling in the Dark: An ABC Theologized.*
San Francisco, CA: HarperOne, 2003.

Campbell, Joseph. *Reflections on the Art of Living: A Joseph Campbell
Companion.* New York, NY: Harper Perennial, 1995.

Cannon, Jay and Chris Bumbaca. "World Series Game 6 interference
call among most controversial in MLB postseason history." *USA
Today,* October 30, 2019. USAToday.com/story/sports/mlb/playoffs
/2019/10/30/world-series-most-controversial-calls-mlb-postseason
-history/4095260002.

Collins, John. *Every Step with Jesus: Following the Saints in the Way
of the Cross.* Huntington, IN: Our Sunday Visitor, 2016.

Flora, Surjit Singh. "Forgive ourselves and forgive others just as God forgives us." International Forgiveness Institute, January 28, 2019. InternationalForgiveness.wordpress.com/category/your -forgiveness-story.

Givey, David W. *The Social Thought of Thomas Merton: The Way of Nonviolence and Peace for the Future*. Winona, MN: Anselm Academic, 2009.

Goodreads. Accessed August 8, 2020. Goodreads.com/quotes/230436 -over-the-years-i-have-come-to-realize-that-the.

Goodreads. Accessed June 10, 2020. Goodreads.com/quotes/7952516 -forgiveness-brings-us-closer-to-those-who-have-hurt-us.

Goodreads. Accessed June 18, 2020. Goodreads.com/quotes/7907646 -you-either-get-bitter-or-you-get-better-it-s-that.

Gottman, John, and Nan Silver. *The Seven Principles for Making Marriage Work*. New York, NY: Harmony Books, 2015.

Hartke, Austin. Nonbinary gender and the diverse beauty of creation. *The Christian Century*. April 16, 2018. ChristianCentury.org/article /critical-essay/nonbinary-gender-and-diverse-beauty-creation.

Hatmaker, Jen. *Of Mess and Moxie: Wrangling Delight Out of This Wild and Glorious Life*. Nashville, TN: Thomas Nelson, 2017.

Jordan, Karin, ed. *The quick theory reference guide: A resource for expert and novice mental health professionals*. Hauppauge, NY: Nova Science Publishers, 2008.

Kaur, Valarie. "Revolutionary Love." Accessed July 7, 2020. ValarieKaur.com/quotes.

King, Jr., Martin Luther. *A Gift of Love: Sermons From Strength to Love and Other Preachings*. Revised ed. Boston, MA: Beacon Press, 2012.

Kingsolver, Barbara. *The Poisonwood Bible*. New York, NY: Harper Perennial, 2002.

Kircanski, Katharina, Matthew D. Lieberman, and Michelle G. Craske. Feelings Into Words: Contributions of Language to Exposure Therapy. *Psychological Science.* 2012; 23 (10): 1086-1091.

Krakauer, Jon. *Into the Wild.* New York, NY: Villard Books, 1996.

Lamott, Anne. *Plan B: Further Thoughts on Faith.* New York, NY: Riverhead Books, 2006.

Lamott, Anne. *Traveling Mercies: Some Thoughts on Faith.* New York, NY: Anchor Books, 2000.

Luchies, Laura B., Eli J. Finkel, James K. McNulty, and Madoka Kumashiro. The Doormat Effect: When Forgiving Erodes Self-Respect and Self-Concept Clarity. *Journal of Personality and Social Psychology,* 2010, 98(5):734-749.

Mandela, Nelson. *Long Walk to Freedom: The Autobiography of Nelson Mandela.* London, England: Abacus, 2013.

McCloud, Melvin. "Angelou." *Shambhala Sun,* January 1988. Hartford-HWP.com/archives/45a/249.html.

McDowell, Crystal. "Favor Isn't Far." Daughters of the Creator, Accessed June 19, 2020. DaughtersOfTheCreator.com/favor-isnt-fair.

Mechthild of Magdeburg and Henry N. Carrigan, ed. *Meditations from Mechthild of Magdeburg.* Orleans, MA: Paraclete Press, 1999.

Merton, Thomas. *My Argument with the Gestapo: Autobiographical novel.* New York, NY: New Directions, 1975.

Merton, Thomas. *Thoughts in Solitude.* New York, NY: Farrar, Straus and Giroux, 2011.

Moore, John Hammond, ed. *The Voice of Small-Town America: The Selected Writings of Robert Quillen, 1920–1948.* Columbia, SC: University of South Carolina Press, 2008.

Morrison, Toni. *Song of Solomon.* New York, NY: Alfred A. Knopf, 1977.

Neff, Kristin. "Self-Compassion." Accessed June 20, 2020. Self-Compassion.org/exercise-4-supportive-touch.

Neff, Kristin. *Self-Compassion: The Proven Power of Being Kind to Yourself.* New York, NY: William Morrow Paperbacks, 2015.

Netton, Ian Richard. *Islam, Christianity and the Mystic Journey: A Comparative Exploration.* Edinburgh, Scotland: Edinburgh University Press, 2011.

Nouwen, Henri J. M. *The Wounded Healer: Ministry in Contemporary Society.* 1st ed. Colorado Springs, CO: Image Books, 1979.

O'Donohue, John. *Anam Cara: A Book of Celtic Wisdom.* New York, NY: HarperCollins, 1998.

Oldenburg, Ray. *The Great Good Place: Cafes, Coffee Shops, Bookstores, Bars, Hair Salons, and Other Hangouts at the Heart of a Community.* 3rd ed. New York, NY: Marlowe & Company, 1999.

Oprah.com "Oprah Talks to Maya Angelou." *O, The Oprah Magazine,* May 2013. Oprah.com/omagazine/maya-angelou-interviewed-by-oprah-in-2013.

Putnam, Robert. *Bowing Alone: The Collapse and Revival of American Community.* 1st ed. New York, NY: Touchstone Books, 2001.

Reed, Marlette B., and Annette M. Lane. *The Meaning Is in the Dirt: Meditations on Life's Richness.* Kindle ed. Winnipeg, Manitoba: Word Alive Press, 2019.

Richards, Stephen. *Forgiveness and Love Conquers All: Healing the Emotional Self.* England: Mirage Publishing, 2011.

Rowling, J. K. *Harry Potter and the Sorcerer's Stone.* Scholastic ed. New York: NY: Scholastic, 1998.

Sbarra, David A., Hillary L. Smith, and Mattias R. Mehl. When Leaving Your Ex, Love Yourself: Observational Ratings of Self-Compassion Predict the Course of Emotional Recovery Following Marital Separation. *Psychological Science* 2012; 23(3):261–269.

Settel, Trudy S., ed. *The Wisdom of Mahatma Gandhi.* Kindle ed. New York, NY: Philosophical Library/Open Road, 2010.

Sittenfeld, Curtis. *Sisterland*. New York, NY: Random House Trade Paperbacks, 2014.

Shapiro, Fred, and Joseph Epstein. *The Yale Book of Quotations*. New Haven, CT: Yale University Press, 2006.

Sontag, Susan. "Piety Without Content." *Against Interpretation and Other Essays*. London, England: Picador, 1961.

Ten Boom, Corrie, and Jamie Buckingham. *Tramp for the Lord*. Assumed 1st ed. Fort Washington, PA: Christian Literature Crusade; 1974.

Underhill, Evelyn. *The Complete Christian Mystic: A Practical, Step-By-Step Guide for Awakening to the Presence of God*. Kindle ed. NewParadigmPress.com, 2010.

Vogt, Manfred, Heinrich Dreesen, and Peter Sundman, eds. *Encounters with Steve de Shazer and Insoo Kim Berg: Inside Stories of Solution-Focused Brief Therapy*. Edinburgh, Scotland: Solutions Books, 2015.

Webster, Patti. *It Happened in Church*. New York, NY: Kensington Books, 2008.

Wilde, Oscar. *Lady Windermere's Fan*. Kindle ed. Mineola, NY: Dover Publications, 2013.

Wong, Kristin. "Why Self-Compassion Beats Self-Confidence." *New York Times*, Dec 28, 2017. NYTimes.com/2017/12/28/smarter-living/why-self-compassion-beats-self-confidence.html.

Wulfhorst, Ellen. "Vietnamese girl burned by napalm focuses on forgiveness in helping U.S. military." *Thomson Reuters Foundation News*, March 22, 2016. News.Trust.org/item/20160322130858-zsfaj.

Yontef, Gary, and Lynne Jacobs. *Gestalt Therapy*. In Raymond J. Corsini and Danny Wedding (Eds.), *Current Psychotherapies*. Belmont, CA: Thomson Higher Education, 2008.

Verse Index

Acknowledgments

The congregation I've served since 2003 has been a profound teacher of forgiveness. When I have stepped on toes or caused hurt, that community of patient souls has been tenaciously loving, offering me the grace to grow up a little more. When my relationship with them has left me bruised or confused, staying in this loving relationship with them has also offered the great gift of growth, leaving my heart always open a little wider and a little more compassionate.

I've learned the art of forgiveness from my hilarious, servant-hearted sister, Rachel, and from my wise mentors and teachers, too many to count, including Carl Bretz, Ken Shuman, and Margaret Marcuson.

I'm grateful to editors Crystal Nero and Bitsy Kemper, for their sharp eyes and clear guidance, and to writing coach Jamie Morris, for her encouraging and challenging faith in me.

My wife, Molly, inspires me with her infinite, principled courage and compassion. To be companions through life is a blessing matched only by the joy of seeing our sons become their own true selves. For all these people and more, for the opportunity to savor this sweet life, and the chance to forgive and be forgiven, again and again, I thank the all-loving God in whose hands is my life.

About the Author

Jake Morrill is a minister, therapist, and leadership coach in East Tennessee. A graduate of Harvard Divinity School and the Iowa Writers' Workshop, and a student of Bowen Family Systems Theory, his previous publications include *Randy Bradley* and *The Cherry Jar*, both works of fiction. For coaching and consulting, his website is JakeMorrill.com.